# TABLE OF CONTENTS

# ACKNOWLEDGMENTS

I give thanks to my great-aunt and grandmother for giving me a good understanding of FAITH and CHARITY. To my parents, thank you for the sacrifices you made in bringing me up to be the man I am today and for giving me a sound foundation and start to life. I also give thanks to all my heroes whom I hold dear to my HEART. These are the people who toiled and strived in the realm of North America and worked to make this world a better place throughout the years!

# INTRODUCTION

Every entrepreneur has recipes for success and tales of overcoming adversity. These recipes and tales serve to articulate each entrepreneur's natural inclination toward the knowledge, perseverance, and patience that are necessary to build and nurture a business. In this regard, *How to Catch a Mouse with No Cheese* is similar to other books written for and by entrepreneurs. This book utilizes my entrepreneurial experiences as launching pads and illustrative devices to demonstrate the grit that is required to open, run, and grow a business. My experiences span the course of 20 years. During that time, I have opened businesses, closed businesses, made millions, and lost millions; I have entrepreneurial war stories that depict true accounts of not only espionage and betrayal, but also the forging of strong alliances. Nevertheless, *How to Catch a Mouse with No Cheese* is distinct from other books written for and by entrepreneurs because it explains how an entrepreneur can start a business without any money. It is designed to serve as a roadmap for anyone with little or no money and who wants to start a business. Moreover, the advice in this book hinges on the reader adhering to the following tenets: (1) faith, (2) truth, (3) self-awareness, (4) self-discipline, and (5) service.

## FAITH

You must have faith to start a business without money. Merriam-Webster Dictionary defines faith as: (1) "firm belief in something for which there is no proof" and (2) "complete trust." I like these definitions of faith because they use the adjectives "firm" and "complete" to describe the level of wholeness and stability that must be present in the hearts and minds of those who profess to have faith that their business ideas and dreams will become reality.

I make this point because some entrepreneurs view faith and optimism as interchangeable parts. Optimism—although useful—by definition is only a *tendency* to expect the best outcome. In times of extreme adversity and disappointment, optimism will wear thin and give way to fear; but faith is *complete* trust and, thus, designed to eradicate fear and self-doubt. In order to be faithful, an entrepreneur must (1) choose faith over fear, (2) identify and ignore the negativity of naysayers, and (3) recognize the lesson in every occurrence.

To start, make a conscious decision on a daily basis to have faith that your business ideas and dreams will not only materialize, but also flourish. I did not do this when I started my first business. At that time, I thought my determination and optimism were sufficient to weather any circumstance. I discovered that determination and optimism were suitable characteristics to possess in cases of moderate adversity or situations that were relatively easy to overcome. Moderate adversity includes, but is not limited to, a lack of training and skills, inadequate business location, inexperienced staff, ineffective marketing strategy, and the inability to formulate a business plan. However, faith is required when you do not have money or any other tangible resources to start your business. The roadblocks will appear endless as well as insurmountable because banks, family, and friends will not loan you money if you do not have any savings, 401(k), or saleable property. In circumstances like these, determination and optimism are eventually overtaken by fear and doubt, but with faith you have a completely different outlook. Faith is complete trust that you will build and grow your business. In essence, faith is the seed of hope that you will water every day.

While you are consciously choosing faith over fear, you must also identify and ignore the negativity of naysayers. Naysayers are people who tell you that you will not achieve your business ideas and dreams. Naysayers may include close relatives, friends, and advisors. They will mask their negativity and doubt in a cloak of constructive criticism. As a result, it is important that you are able to distinguish between negativity and constructive criticism. Remember that the goal of negativity is to cast doubt and demoralize. In most instances, naysayers will either make obvious or well-known statements and/or present you with cynical questions. For example, a naysayer may state, "You do not know anything about starting and running a business. It is extremely difficult, and very few businesses succeed." Others may frame these negative opinions as questions: "Do you know anything about starting or running a business? Do you know that it extremely difficult and very few businesses succeed?" Moreover, persistent naysayers will go a step beyond presenting you with obvious or well-known statements and/or cynical questions. They will offer alternatives to your business ideas and dreams. They will tell you about fields that offer you job security. They will encourage you to go back to school. Overall, they will challenge your faith in your business ideas and dreams. On the other hand, yeasayers will offer constructive criticism in a manner that supports your business goals. Yeasayers want you to achieve your dreams. They may recognize your deficiencies. However, unlike the naysayers, they will make suggestions and offer solutions that are line with your desire to start a business. Specifically, yeasayers may connect you with successful entrepreneurs, buy you a book on starting a business, offer you resources, suggest relevant webinars and/or workshops, or introduce you to community leaders. Identify and ignore the negativity of naysayers. Otherwise, you may risk losing faith in your ability to open, run, and grow a business.

In addition to choosing faith over fear and identifying and ignoring the negativity of naysayers, you must recognize the lessons in every occurrence and encounter in order to be faithful. Successful entrepreneurs learn from their experiences as well as the experiences of others. They analyze every event, looking for common threads that produce desirable results as well as practices that promote setbacks. In order to recognize the lesson in every occurrence and encounter, practice the art of being alert. This simply means that all of your senses are fully engaged in the moment. Your mind is focused on the event at hand. It could be an interaction you have with a customer, employee, banker, or consultant. It could be your observations of interactions that key players like customers, employees, bankers, and consultants are having with others that guide your future. You may be at a workshop or logged into a webinar. Whatever the scenario, refrain from focusing on what has happened in the past or what might happen in the future in order to fully reap the benefits of the present. Later, during quiet time and reflection, you can contemplate how the experience compares to other events, and what lessons are to be learned. You may find it helpful to record these lessons in a journal. This will allow you to revisit the lessons often as inspiration or customized tutorials. To help recognize the lessons in every occurrence and encounter, you may find it useful to focus on the events that led up to the outcome. Note all of the circumstances that played a role in the encounter, including, but not limited to, the time of day (morning, afternoon, or evening) and year (e.g., winter, spring, summer, or fall), the setting (e.g., noisy restaurant, upscale hotel meeting room, or a crowded boardroom), the people involved, any verbal cues (e.g., What was said, how was it said, what words were used, was the response appropriate, could the response be improved in the future to yield a better result and if so, how?), non-verbal cues (e.g., consistent eye contact, unfolded arms, constantly looking away, texting, taking phone calls, smiling, laughter, or deep sighs), and preparedness (Were you adequately prepared? If so, how? If not, what more could you have done?). These steps will help you recognize and learn the lessons from every occurrence and encounter in order to remain faithful to your business ideas and dreams.

## TRUTH

You must be truthful to start a business without money. In order to be truthful, you must possess strong personal integrity. Personal integrity involves a high ethical standard or moral value system that dictates how you interact with others. Often times, American cinema and television will depict successful business people as ruthless liars and cheaters who always win. In the real world, these ruthless liars and cheaters eventually end up in jail or out a lot of money. Personal integrity will serve as a great asset when you begin to develop business relationships in your market area. If you are honest in your dealings with people, then your reputation as an ethical entrepreneur will grow. This type of reputation will be paramount as you seek to establish yourself as an expert in your industry and build a customer base. Therefore, become truthful in your personal and professional interactions with others by (1) taking inventory of your belief system, (2) addressing weaknesses in your moral code, and (3) adopting honesty as your default setting.

The first step in becoming truthful is to take inventory of your belief system. Start by outlining the basic principles that define your belief system. Your belief system may be based on a religion, culture, secular philosophy, or other influence. If your belief system includes honesty and respect for others and yourself, then you should consistently practice your belief system, evaluating your business practices to ensure that they are in line with your belief system. On the other hand, if your belief system tolerates dishonesty and low personal integrity, then you will be served well to seek and embrace a belief system that promotes high personal integrity. Otherwise, short-term profit gained through deceptive practices and scams will be inevitably overshadowed by media scandals and public distrust for you and your brand.

Next, address weaknesses in your moral code. You should be acutely aware of your ethical shortcomings and work to improve them. Examine your storehouse of experiences and interactions with others throughout your daily life at home, work, and in public spaces. Determine the circumstances during which you are most likely to practice dishonesty. You may find that you are prone to dishonesty when you feel cornered, pressured, or stressed, or when you observe that others are particularly weak and gullible., You may even discover that you are dishonest in all of your interactions with others. Dishonesty indicates unresolved insecurities and fears in a person. Some insecurities and fears that deal with lack of training or experience can be overcome with a plan to gain the appropriate skills and experience necessary to become a leader in your industry. Other personal insecurities and fears such as addictions, disabilities, and personality disorder will require the help of professional counselors and healthcare providers. Whatever the case, address the weaknesses in your moral code by identifying them and correcting them.

Finally, adopt honesty as your default setting in business. It is simply easier and more beneficial to tell the truth. The truth may not always lead to instant gratification, but it will create a sustainable path upon which your business can grow and thrive. If you build your business by lying to your customers, employees, vendors, and partners, then you will have created a foundation made of a highly corrosive material. So, no matter how beautiful the business appears to be, you will know that at any moment your dishonesty will be revealed, serving to erode valuable relationships, your reputation, and the viability of your brand. Tell the truth.


## SELF-AWARENESS

You must possess self-awareness to start a business without money. What makes you tick? There are myriad considerations when starting a business: (1) obtaining licenses and permits; (2) ordering equipment and supplies; (3) hiring and training support staff; (4) working with vendors and consultants; (5) paying bills; (6) establishing and adhering to a budget; (7) marketing and selling; (6) satisfying customers; (7) developing the brand; and the list goes on and on. In the beginning, without any money, you will be charged with doing all the work. Thus, you must be aware of who you are as person in order to get a great deal accomplished with you as your primary resource. Some may say that you do not know who you really are until you are placed in a specific situation. In some fields this may be true, but this is not the case in business. As you travel the road to starting a business without any money, your personal attributes become immediately apparent. It is better to assess yourself and come to terms with yourself prior to diving head first into starting a business. By doing this, you will be better equipped to tailor your activities and responsibilities in a way that will yield better results. In order to achieve strong self-awareness you must acknowledge and respond to your natural temperament, emotions, and motivations.

In an effort to gain strong self-awareness, begin by understanding your natural temperament and what it means to possess that temperament. Business involves an enormous amount of interpersonal communication. Consequently, it matters if you are an introvert or extrovert, deliberate or impulsive, calm or emotional, relaxed or nervous. It is important that you, as an entrepreneur, know the strengths and weaknesses associated with your temperament in order to properly prepare for less than ideal situations and, when possible, coordinate events and exchanges in a manner that are better suited for your temperament. If you are aware of your temperament, then you can establish efficient systems that speak to the way that you work best. If you are an introvert, this may mean that you will establish a system of communicating with key people that involves more emails and text messages rather than face-to-face conferences. On the other hand, if you are an extrovert, then you may find it advantageous to conduct in-person interviews. I am simplifying temperament for the purpose of this introduction. It is important to note that temperament usually falls somewhere on a continuum between two extremes. Nevertheless, if you are aware of your temperament, then it will allow you the foresight to prepare for—or even avoid—certain situations as well as the freedom to tailor systems and circumstances within your realm of control.

You must also know what triggers your emotions in order to have strong self-awareness. Emotions include—but are not limited to—joy, anger, love, hatred, disgust, resentment, affection, attraction, euphoria, and shame.

Emotions are often triggered by outside stimuli and are revealed through physical expressions and chemical reactions in the brain. In business, as in all facets of life, emotions occur naturally. As an entrepreneur, as much as possible, avoid being caught off guard by your emotions. As a result, you may find it beneficial to act out various hypothetical situations in your mind in order to frame an appropriate response. Similarly, if you know that you are easy to anger or cry when consuming alcohol, then you may consider limiting alcohol consumption or refraining altogether in business settings.

Finally, you must know what motivates you in order to acquire strong self-awareness. Determine what is motivating you to start a business. It may be a desire to be your own boss, gain financial stability, have more personal flexibility, pursue your passion, or any combination of these. It is important to know what motivates you because these factors can produce positive behaviors like drive and focus, as well as negative behavior like dishonesty. You can use this information to make ethical business decisions that will speak to your desires and work to your advantage.


## SELF-DISCIPLINE

You must have self-discipline in order to start a business without money. It is not enough to have a great idea. You must also follow through and take action. You must adhere to deadlines and meet goals within a specific timeframe if you intend to build a successful business. Presumably, your competitors are in the trenches making positive things happen for themselves. If you lack self-discipline, then you are not a competitor because you are absent (or most often absent) from the action. The path to building self-discipline involves: (1) creating and following a daily routine; (2) creating and following a business plan; and (3) holding yourself accountable.

To develop self-discipline, you should create and follow a daily routine. Begin by creating a detailed schedule that accounts for every minute of your day, from the time you wake up until the time you retire for the day. As an entrepreneur, since you will not be doing the same thing each day, it is important to see where and how you are spending your time. This vital information that will help you make effective decisions and adjustments in your time management. For example, suppose you create and adhere to a planned schedule for a month. Then, at the end of the month, you assess how you are spending your time. You notice that you spend 90% of your time developing daily operating systems and researching technology that the business will need and just 10% networking with potential vendors. At this point, you may realize that you are neglecting marketing and brand building opportunities. As a result, you make the necessary adjustments to your schedule to build in time for marketing and building brand awareness. Without a schedule, this type of information may go unnoticed for months.

In addition to creating and following a daily routine to build self-discipline, it is also essential to create and follow a working business plan that not only defines the future of the business, but also delineates short-term and long-term goals for sales, customer service, marketing, and staffing. This may be drafted most effectively in terms of year-one goals, year-three goals, and year-five goals. You should map out step-by-step plans for reaching your goals. Do not view the working business plan as a hard and fast document. Instead, update it as new developments occur. Also, the working business plan does not have to be 100 pages to be valuable. As an internal document, you can use brief notes and bulleted points as long as you understand them and can decipher them later.

Lastly, if you want to form greater self-discipline, then you must hold yourself accountable when your business suffers due to your lack of self-discipline. Missing deadlines, failing to return phone calls, and ignoring numerous other responsibilities will harm the potential growth of your business. After acknowledging your lack of self-discipline, then take action by recommitting yourself to adhering to your daily schedule and working business plan.


## SERVICE

You must commit to serving others when you are starting a business without money. Starting a business without money can be challenging and yet gratifying. You will realize that you have a great deal to offer in terms of service to others. Accordingly, reach out to your local and/or global community to determine where you can do the most good. By serving others, you hone your leadership skills, meet people outside of your industry, and maintain a healthy level of humility and kindness.

Throughout *How to Catch a Mouse with No Cheese*, I expose my journey to embrace the principles of faith, truth, self-awareness, self-discipline, and service. For years now, I have followed these principles as a way of life and have reaped financial, psychological, and emotional rewards as a result. I can only hope that this book will be the start of your journey to successful business ownership and lasting self-fulfillment.

# CHAPTER ONE:
# NO MONEY, NO PROBLEM

*"TRUE FAITH in YOUR FATHER IN HEAVEN is the only way to make your BUSINESS DREAMS come TRUE when you are starting with nothing in a HELL HOLE."*

At the beginning of my senior year in college, I started a business with no money. It began with a phone call from my older brother. During the call, he informed me that our father would no longer provide me with financial support. My father would no longer pay my bills or send me money. The call was not a warning or a heads up to get my ducks in a row, but rather a harsh alarm signifying that all financial support ceased as of the moment my brother had called. Initially, I cried uncontrollably because I was distraught and hurt beyond words. I was a full-time student with a year of coursework to complete before graduating. I did not have any money. I did not have any savings. I did not have good credit.

After I received the call from my brother, I prayed and asked God to help me. Thankfully, God answered my prayers the next day. My faith had cleared a path for me to think without the clutter associated with fear. The wheels in my brain were turning rapidly and productively. I was officially on the road to starting a business. Since I did not have money, I needed to start a business that fit with the resources and assets I had.

I immediately took inventory of my non-monetary resources and assets, thinking:

- My father will not give me money, but he, along with my other family members, will certainly support me in other ways.

- My sister is a lawyer, and I have brothers who have started successful businesses. They will provide services and consulting that I will need. Even if they would be unwilling to provide me their services for free, they will wait until I am making money to require payment.

- My mother and father are active, well-regarded community and business leaders. They own and operate an outpatient mental health clinic that provides counseling services to low-income children and adolescents. These children and adolescents receive Medicaid benefits and have been diagnosed with developmental delays and/or an attention deficit disorder. In this business, my father is positioned as an authority because he has served as an educator, supervisor, and political figure in the community for 30 years.

- My parents help many people in the community. So, I have the good name and goodwill that my family has built in our community over the years.

- I will earn a Bachelor of Science in Psychology degree in the near future.

- I am determined, driven, and willing to commit to going to school on a full-time basis and commuting back home on the weekends to run the business.

- I will carve out time between attending classes and completing coursework to conduct research and complete paperwork that will be necessary to get the business started.

Given the resources I had available to me at the time, I decided that it made sense for me to start a part-time business in my hometown. The business would offer services that were complementary to those offered by my mother and father's business. My business would offer outpatient substance abuse counseling services to low-income adolescents who received Medicaid benefits and, as a result of their substance-abuse issues, were exhibiting behavior problems at home and school. I knew there was tremendous demand for the services that my business would offer because I witnessed it in my mother and father's business. Many parents in the community had children who were abusing prescription drugs used for attention deficit disorders as well as marijuana. The youth required counseling in an effort to help them make better choices and stop abusing drugs. I viewed this business model as the most practical for me to start with no money because Medicaid paid approved providers on a weekly basis. This payment schedule would allow me to provide clients with services, pay myself a salary, pay my staff, and pay the other expenses associated with running the business.

Before I could actually start the business, I had to perform research, complete paperwork, and obtain approval from Medicaid. To start, I visited my state's department of hospitals' website to become an approved provider. From the website, I was able to select adolescent substance-abuse counseling as the service I would provide in my business. Soon after, I learned that in order to serve as an approved Medicaid provider, I would need to develop a current operations manual as well as a set of rules and regulation that were Medicaid compliant. As a result, I reached out to my sister, who is a lawyer, for assistance in customizing an operations manual as well as a rules and regulation document. With her help I had an effective operations manual as well as documented rules and regulations within a couple of weeks. Both documents were developed at no upfront costs. By following Medicaid guidelines, I obtained my license as an approved Medicaid provider with relative ease.

Around the time I became an approved and licensed provider for Medicaid, my father closed his outpatient mental health clinic and focused on his work in our community's school system. This meant that there was an opportunity for me to take over his office space and obtain his equipment with no money down. I talked to my father and he agreed to let me use all of his equipment – file cabinets, computers, desks, telephones, chairs, etc. He and I agreed that I would pay him for the equipment once I began to make money. Along the same line, I spoke to the landlord of my father's old business space. I told him my business plan and explained that I did not have money for the first month's rent. The landlord and I came to contractual terms that included him waiving the first month's rent. Once I secured the location, a Medicaid regulator came out to audit my business. Soon after the audit was complete, I was approved to begin services. I reached this point about a month after I received "the call" from my brother.

It is important to note that at the time I started my business as an approved Medicaid provider, Medicaid did not require preauthorization from the state in order for approved providers to perform services. A parent had the freedom to call an approved provider and seek services. Under these conditions, I carried out aggressive community outreach efforts and found a licensed physician to perform independent evaluations of youth. I knocked on doors and spoke at community venues like religious institutions and charitable organizations, introducing my services and myself to the community. As I initially estimated, the marketing process was made easier because the people in the community were familiar with me and knew how my family conducted business (i.e., ethically and in the best interest of clients).

My marketing efforts paid off. Upon opening my doors, there was a flood of parents waiting in line with their children. They had arrived for a prescreening evaluation and to be seen by the physician. My staff worked non-stop for the entire day. Many of the youth who were prescreened and seen by the physician were ultimately approved for services. It was intense and rewarding, but most importantly, I had started my first business, Community Case Management, with no money.


## LESSONS AND CAVEATS

The circumstances and details surrounding my experiences of starting a business with no money are unique. They are not only unique because they centered on what was going on in my life at the time, but also because many of the opportunities that were present at the time do not exist today. As a result, the gems of wisdom that must be sifted from my experience are the embedded lessons that apply to any situation where a person is embarking on a quest to start a business with no money.


### Lesson #1—List Your Non-Monetary Assets

Acknowledge that you do not have money to start a business. However, do not place great emphasis on what you do not have. Concentrate on making a list of your non-monetary assets. For the purpose of this book, non-monetary assets encompass anything or anybody that can help you achieve your goal of starting a business with no money. As a result, non-monetary assets come in the following forms:

- *People*—There are two criteria that a person must meet in order to be considered a non-monetary assets:

    1. They must possess something of value (time, money, expertise, advice, talents, tools/equipment, etc.) that they are willing to give you to start your business.

    2. They must be willing to give you those things of value for the advancement of your business on the terms of no payment or delayed payment.

    People that you should consider as non-monetary assets are people within your network with whom you share a connection, interest, and some familiarity. These people include, but are not limited to, family, friends, community leaders (entrepreneurs and politicians), religious leaders, teachers (former and current), coaches (former and current), and mentors.

- *Talents*—If you were born with certain abilities and predispositions, then you should count them as non-monetary assets. It may be the case that you are naturally driven, determined, analytical, outspoken, punctual, or detail-oriented. Any characteristic that you have a habit of exhibiting that can be used productively is a non-monetary asset.

- *Skills*—Abilities that you have cultivated through education, practice, hard work and perseverance are non-monetary assets. For example, you may be skilled in cooking, building, sewing, dancing, singing, or inventing. Similarly, you may have a degree or certification in a particular field. Whatever the skill may be, list it.

## Lesson #2—Maximize Your Non-Monetary Assets

After you list your non-monetary assets, then determine how you can maximize their usefulness. An effective way to accomplish this is by creating a checklist of tasks that must be addressed and completed when starting a business. Once you create the checklist, you will have a better sense of how to best utilize your non-monetary assets. A sample checklist follows on the next page.

# CHECKLIST

| PRIORITY | DUE DATE | WHAT | NON-MONETARY ASSET UTILIZED | COMPLETED |
|---|---|---|---|---|
| | | Create a business plan | | |
| | | Choose a Business Type and structure | | |
| | | Obtain Licenses, Permits, and/or Certifications | | |
| | | Register a Business Name | | |
| | | Obtain a Tax Identification Number | | |
| | | Find and Secure a Site | | |
| | | Negotiate the Lease | | |
| | | Obtain Equipment and Supplies | | |
| | | Draft an Operations Manual | | |
| | | Create/Obtain Relevant Forms | | |
| | | Obtain Insurance | | |
| | | Establish Telephone Service | | |
| | | Establish Internet Service | | |
| | | Set up utilities | | |
| | | Determine Staffing Needs | | |

| | | | | |
|---|---|---|---|---|
| | | Market | | |
| | | Sell | | |
| | | Network | | |
| | | Determine Staffing Needs | | |
| | | Recruit and Hire Staff | | |
| | | Train Staff | | |
| | | Create Daily Operating Procedures | | |
| | | Obtain business cards and brochures | | |
| | | Open for Business | | |

After you decide how you will utilize your non-monetary assets, then contact the people on your list and share your business plans with them. In this day of advanced technology, it may seem reasonable to make contact via email or text. However, the initial contact should be a face-to-face meeting, video call, or voice call. Be direct and specific when articulating the help you need. For example, you might say, "I need you to help me create my business plan." During the initial contact, obtain confirmation that they are willing to help you AND that they will either help you for free or wait until your business is up and running to receive payment.


## CAVEATS

In addition to the lessons that are detailed above, there are a few caveats associated with my experience of starting a business with no money that should be explicitly stated and explained. I was tremendously blessed to have had the resources, determination, and drive to open a profitable business in a relatively short amount of time. Nevertheless, you should be aware of the disadvantages associated with working with family or friends, starting a business that is reliant on public sector funding, and starting a business too quickly.

To start, you should be careful when making the decision to work closely with family or friends. I have a successful mentor who does not do business with either family members or friends. He justifies this practice by quoting the proverb: "Familiarity breeds contempt." Roughly translated, this proverb means that you lose admiration for family members and friends when you work together for a long time. I respect the sentiment of the proverb and encourage entrepreneurs, when possible, to fulfill their staffing needs with qualified referrals that are not relatives or friends. With that said, there are times when working with family and friends is in your best interest. For example, when I started my first business with no money, I did not have a lot of options or time. I had to utilize the non-monetary assets within my grasp. This meant that I had to work with family members and close friends. Unfortunately, in the beginning I did not know the value of establishing healthy workplace rules and boundaries for my staff, who were also my relatives and friends. Without established rules and boundaries, professional limitations were—more often than not—stretched, blurred, or completely ignored. This type of behavior led to some of my relationships with family and friends being irreparably damaged. If I had put limits and guidelines in place during the early stages of starting my first business, then it would have set a positive tone and, at the very least, given the entire team a chance to settle into their professional roles. You can achieve this by creating an employee handbook that delineates key human resources policies that are compliant with both local, state, and federal laws and regulations. Topics in an employee handbook may include, but are not limited to, the following:

- Local Employment Laws
- Handbook Receipt Procedures
- Client Service Guidelines
- Mission Statement
- Vision Statement
- Training Period
- Dress Code
- Grooming and Hygiene
- Business Hours
- Work Schedule
- Employee Paperwork
- Attendance
- Drugs and Alcohol in the Workplace
- Accidents and Emergency Situations • Crime and Robbery
- Fire Protection
- Computer, Email, and Internet Usage
- Telephone Usage

- Evaluations
- Promotions
- Transfers
- Resignations
- Equal Employment Opportunities
- Policy Against Discrimination and Harassment
- Policy Against Sexual Harassment
- Complaint Procedures
- Pay Procedure
- Time Reporting
- Payroll Checks
- Payroll Deductions
- Change Of Address
- Lost Paychecks
- Employee Meals
- Employee Breaks
- Break Areas
- Vacation
- Bereavement Leave
- Maternity Leave
- Military Leave
- Time Off to Vote
- Jury Duty and Witness
- Meetings
- Teamwork
- Communication
- Smoking
- Visitors at Work
- Personal Belongings
- Cell Phones
- Solicitation Policy
- Care of Equipment
- Employee Board
- Disciplinary Procedures

Once you have policies and procedures in place, you must not only enforce them, but also adhere to them.

Secondly, there are disadvantages to starting a business that is solely or primarily reliant on public funding. The biggest disadvantage is that the public programs that fund your services can be reduced or eliminated with little or no notice to you. Moreover, even if the programs that fund your services are not reduced or limited, the state or federal government can arbitrarily decide to remove you as an approved provider and, effectively, close your business. This is exactly what happened to me. My business was solely reliant on Medicaid, a form of public funding. So, when the state decided that I could not be an approved provider, I did not have a leg on which to stand. Not long after that incident, I made the decision that if I opened another business that was solely dependent on public funding, then my goal—from the onset—would be to get out of the public-sector business as quickly as possible by selling the public sector business and starting another comparable business in the private sector.

Finally, starting a business with no money in a relatively short amount of time may cost you a lot of money later. I started my first business approximately a month after my brother called me to say that my father would no longer provide me with financial support. Without question, I was motivated by a sense of urgency to have the means to support myself. I decided that I would open as quickly as I could and, eventually, go back and work out any details I may have missed or neglected. As it turns out, that was a costly strategy insofar as professionals (lawyers and accountants, specifically) charge more to solve problems than they do to avoid them. Today, in addition to seeking professional advice, I analyze and research my business issues to ensure that the advice I am receiving is the most sound and appropriate for my purposes.

# CHAPTER TWO:
# BUSINESS INDUSTRY AND TYPE MATTER

## *Faith ♦ Truth ♦ Self-Awareness ♦ Self-Determination ♦ Service*

Approximately four years after I opened my first business, Community Case Management, with no money, the state arbitrarily shut my business down. Not long after the state closed my business, I decided to use some of the profits I had earned to start a candy manufacturing and distribution company. My candy business was well received by local stores; but the politics associated with the candy manufacturing and distribution industry in the target market area I chose were horrible. Consequently, about a year into the candy manufacturing and distribution business, I realized that it simply was not a sustainable business model. I closed the candy business and returned the equipment and supplies to the vendor in order to recover some of the money I had lost. For several years after I closed my candy business, I dwelled in a metaphorical wilderness. I had no money, no savings, and no credit. I was living with my then girlfriend because I could not afford a home of my own. I was humiliated by my circumstances. So, I became despondent and bitter.

As God would have it, I would once again be placed on the road to starting a business with no money. This time, the catalyst was a phone call from my younger brother. He was looking for someone to partner with to start a non-medical, in-home healthcare company that focused on elder care and support. I explained to him that I did not have any money to partner with him. Nevertheless, he recognized the value that I could bring to the concept. He knew that I had built a business from nothing and would be able to bring a great deal of know-how to the business. With this in mind, he loaned me $1,500.00 to become his partner. With that partnership agreement, A Plus

Home Care Services was born.

Today, I realize that there were larger lessons that I had to learn from losing my first business. Two of the most significant lessons are that the business industry and structure you select really matter when starting a business with no money.

## BUSINESS INDUSTRIES OVERVIEW

What business industry can you enter with no money? The answer to this question matters when you are starting a business with no money. There are a multitude of business industries from which to choose and—by default—they are all sales businesses because you must sell a product or service in order to make money. This book focuses on three broad industry categories: retail, restaurant, and service.

## Retail

Retail businesses involve selling goods directly to consumers. There are numerous initial-investment costs associated with getting started in the retail industry. These costs are not only expensive, but also necessary if you want to increase your chances of being successful and becoming profitable in the retail industry. This is the case even with E-commerce retail businesses. In order to become profitable in E-commerce, you need to drive traffic to your site (which costs money) and build brand awareness through various marketing platforms (which also costs money) so that consumers will visit your site and purchase your goods. These initial-investment costs include, but are not limited to, the following:

### Brand Development and Marketing

- Brand Name Development
- Trademark Registration (Legal Services)
- Logo Design and Development (Design Services)
- Interior and Exterior Signage and Décor
- Marketing Collateral Printing (Business Cards, Direct Mail Pieces,

Letterhead, Etc.)
- Website Development and Domain Registration (Website Designer)
- Miscellaneous Marketing Expenses, including Grand Opening Event Budget

## Operating Expenditures

- Business Licenses and Permits
- Deposit to Secure a Rental Lease
- Advance Rent Payments
- Security Deposits for Utilities and Services
- Inventory
- Insurance
- Business Accounts
- Office Equipment
- Cash Register (or Point of Sale System)
- Cleaning Supplies
- Technical Support
- Personnel

## Site Renovation

- Construction
- Equipment, Fixtures, Supplies and Tools

## Restaurant

Restaurant businesses involve selling and serving meals and refreshments directly to consumers. Like the retail industry, there are numerous initial-investment costs associated with getting started in the restaurant industry. The costs are not only expensive, but some goods are also perishable. This means that not only are you spending lots of money, but also it is highly likely that some of it will go to waste. This would be the case even if you opened a small hotdog stand. These initial-investment costs include, but are not limited to, the following:

## Brand Development and Marketing

- Brand Name Development
- Trademark Registration (Legal Services)
- Logo Design and Development (Design Services)
- Interior and Exterior Signage and Décor
- Marketing Collateral Printing (Business Cards, Flyers, Menus, Coupons, Etc.)
- Website Development and Domain Registration (Website Designer)
- Miscellaneous Marketing Expenses, including Grand Opening Event Budget

## Operating Expenditures

- Business Licenses and Permits
- Food Safety Classes and Coursework
- Deposit to Secure a Rental Lease
- Advance Rent Payments
- Security Deposits for Utilities and Services
- Initial Order of Food and Beverages
- Insurance
- Business Accounts
- Office Equipment
- Cash Register (or Point of Sale System)
- Cleaning Supplies
- Technical Support
- Personnel

## Site Renovation

- Construction

- Furniture, Equipment, Fixtures, Supplies and Tools
- Smallwares (Tableware, Dishes, Utensils, etc.)

## Service

Services businesses involve offering and performing services that benefit customers. Unlike the retail and restaurant industries, you can start with no money. All you need is a skill-set, determination, and the ability to let customers know that you have skills and know-how that can benefit them. Moreover, it is customary in certain sectors of the service industry for customers to pay you a partial or complete payment in advance of providing the service. For example, if you possess culinary skills, then you might decide to become a personal chef for busy professionals. For absolutely zero dollars you can begin to spread the word about your services by telling anyone and everyone you know. You might create a presence on social media and/or start a blog about the benefits of freshly prepared foods. At this point, all you need to start is just one customer. Depending on your business model, you can receive payment before you prepare a meal as well as use your customer's space, equipment, and food to prepare the meals. Of course, this is just one example. On the other hand, maybe you are an artist. You might decide to design custom murals for infant nurseries and children's rooms. For absolutely zero dollars you can draw some sample sketches that demonstrate your level of talent and creativity. Then, you network with professional interior designers, tell everyone you know the services you offer, and create a presence on social media. Again, all you need is just one customer to get started. Depending on your business model, you can receive all or some percentage of your fee before you begin work on the mural and then pass on all costs for paints, brushes, and other supplies to the customer.

I strongly recommend that entrepreneurs with no money start a business in the service industry. The service industry focuses on the skills and talents you possess as opposed to the resources that you lack.

## BUSINESS STRUCTURES OVERVIEW

When I first started a business with no money, I structured my business as an S corporation without realizing the advantages and disadvantages associated with this type of business. As it turned out, I should never have structured my business as an S corporation because it requires the establishment of a board of directors, and you (the owner?) must meet with the board of directors regularly. Based on my goals at the time, I should have structured my business as a limited liability company. Eventually, I paid dearly for my lack of judgment and failure to research.

There are six business structures that you may consider. They include: (1) sole proprietorship; (2) limited liability company; (3) cooperative; (4) corporation; (5) partnership; and (6) S corporation. For this discussion, I will define each business structure and list a few of their key advantages and disadvantages. I strongly suggest that you talk to qualified professionals before selecting a business structure.

## Sole Proprietorship

A sole proprietorship is the easiest and most frequently established business structure when starting a business. Under this structure you are the business, and the business is you; there is no distinction. As a result, you have a right to all the business' profits and are personally responsible for all the business' financial obligations, legal liabilities, and costs.

| SOLE PROPRIETORSHIP | |
|---|---|
| **PROS** | **CONS** |
| Simple and cost effective to create | Limitless personal liability |
| Absolute control | Absolute control |
| Stress-free accounting and tax preparation | Hard to get investors and banks to give money |

## Limited Liability Company

A limited liability company (LLC) offers the limited liability aspects of a corporation as well as tax and operational benefits of a partnership. Every state has its own rules and guidelines for establishing an LLC. Most of these rules and guidelines will impact how you perform the following tasks:

- Selecting a business name
- Filing the articles of organization
- Developing an operating agreement
- Securing licenses and permits
- Recruiting and hiring employees
- Publicizing your business

| LIMITED LIABILITY COMPANY | |
| --- | --- |
| **PROS** | **CONS** |
| Limited personal liability | Must pay self-employment taxes |
| Comparatively minimal recordkeeping and paperwork | Law and guidelines vary greatly from state to state |
| Minimal limitations on profit sharing | Prohibited from taking advantage of incentive stock options, engaging in tax-free reorganizations, or issuing Section 1244 stock |

## Cooperative

A cooperative business structure is owned by and operated for the advantage of the individuals using the service. The members of the cooperative are entitled to the profits and earnings of the cooperative. Unlike other business structures, in order to form a cooperative, prospective members must first come together and agree on a mutual need as well as a plan on how to satisfy that need. Then, an organizing committee performs investigative meetings, surveys, and feasibility studies. These items must be completed prior to every member signing off on the business plan.

Cooperatives are not required to incorporate. In the event that you choose to incorporate your cooperative, then you must adhere to state-specific laws that speak to the following topics:

- Registering articles of incorporation
- Establishing bylaws
- Developing a membership application
- Performing a charter member meeting and electing directors
- Securing licenses and permits
- Hiring employees

| COOPERATIVE | |
| --- | --- |
| **PROS** | **CONS** |
| Only taxed Once on your income | Difficult to secure money from investors |
| Eligible for government-sponsored grant programs | Dependent on membership participation |
| Ability to leverage size in return for better prices, goods, and services | |
| Members can come and go without disrupting the business | |
| Structured as a pure democracy - one vote per member | |

## Corporation

More multifaceted and intricate than other business structures, a corporation (which is also referred to as a C corporation) is an autonomous legal entity that is owned by shareholders. Moreover, these shareholders are not held liable for the deeds the corporation carries out and/or the debts the corporation acquires. Instead, the corporation is solely responsible.

Each state has its own laws and regulations that govern establishing a corporation.

| CORPORATION | |
| --- | --- |
| **PROS** | **CONS** |
| Ability to sell ownership shares through stock offerings/generate capital | Expensive and time-consuming to establish and run |
| Reduced personal liability | Extensive paperwork |
| Owners file taxes separately from the corporation | Expensive administrative fees |
| Potential to attract better talent because of benefits and stock options | Cumbersome tax and legal requirements (potential for double tax) |

## Partnership

A partnership is one business in which two or more people share ownership. Partners share in the profits and losses of the business. Given the complexity of partnerships, it is highly recommended that all facets of the business are discussed, addressed, and written into a legal agreement, which the partners will sign. Some key issues that should be spelled out in the legal document include:

- Dividing profits
- Resolving disputes
- Altering ownership/Bringing in new and/or additional partners
- Buying out current partners
- Ending the partnership

The three types of partnerships that can be established include:

- General Partnerships

  - Assumes that profits, liability, and operational responsibilities are shared equally between the partners. Otherwise, the percentages must be articulated in the legal agreement.

- Limited Partnerships

  - Permits partners to possess limited liability as well as limited involvement regarding business decisions.

- Joint Ventures

  - Functions as a general partnership for a limited time or for a specific project.

| PARTNERSHIP | |
| --- | --- |
| **PROS** | **CONS** |
| Comparatively simple and cost effective | Great potential for disagreements |
| Shared risk, liability, and responsibility | Shared risk and liability |
| Synergistic skills, talents, and knowledge | Shared profits |

## S Corporation

An S corporation (which is also referred to as an S Corp) is a specific type of corporation that is established via an IRS tax election. Prior to forming an S Corp, a business must qualify under IRS stipulations. Establishment of an S Corp allows qualifying corporations to avoid double taxation.

The S Corp is different from a standard corporation insofar as:

- Profits and losses can impact your personal tax return
- Shareholders are taxed
- Shareholder who works for the business must be compensated based on fair market value or run the risk of IRS reclassification

| S CORPORATION | |
|---|---|
| **PROS** | **CONS** |
| Save on taxes | Required director and shareholder conferences, documentation from those meetings, adoption and revisions to bylaws, stock transfers, and records maintenance |
| Can write off certain business expenses | Shareholders must be paid a salary that is indicative of their fair market value (anything too low or too high are consider red flags and grounds for IRS reclassification) |
| Business exist independently of shareholders | |

# CHAPTER THREE:
# CONSIDER THE END FROM THE BEGINNING

## *Faith ♦ Truth ♦ Self-Awareness ♦ Self-Determination ♦ Service*

When I started my first business with no money, I did not know the benefits of thinking about an end goal or exit strategy at the start of creating my business. Many businesses fail because they lack a plan that defines a strategy for making it to the end. When I started, I was completely focused on my personal survival; what could I do to make money in order to buy food, keep a roof over my head, and pay my bills? I knew that starting at the bottom was extremely difficult. So, the odds were already against me. This mindset proved to be a self-fulfilling prophecy insofar as I chose the wait-and-see exit strategy, which simply means that I did nothing to plan my exit from the business. Ultimately, the wait-and-see exit strategy proved detrimental to me because I lost my business to a forced exit. I had not planned. In essence, I relinquished control over how I would exit my business to an outside entity that did not care about my business or my future.

Upon opening my second business with no money, I knew that I had to plan my transition from running a business that was dependent on public funding to establishing a business that was part of the open market. The second time around, I planned my exit strategy from the beginning. Each of my business decisions—whether brand building, tax considerations, or plans for increasing revenue—were made with my exit strategy in mind. Ultimately, my exit strategy involved starting a new, similar business that only catered to private-pay clients as well as finding a third-party buyer for the business that relied on government funding.

When starting a business with no money, you should think about your end goal or exit strategy in the beginning stages of establishing your business.

Keep in mind that as your business evolves, so should your exit strategy plans. Contemplate the following when choosing an exit strategy:

- Do you want to retire or start a new venture? If so, when?

- Do you have someone that you want to take over the business?

- How much money will you need to live independently or start another business when you exit?

- What can you do now to limit your future tax liability?

Although exit strategies for businesses can take on many forms and often rely on timing rather than a specific end date, there are seven (not counting wait-and-see) common exit strategies: (1) transfer ownership and management to family or close friends; (2) sell to employees or partners; (3) sell to a third-party outsider; (4) go public; (5) get acquired; (6) drain the business; and (7) liquidate.

## TRANSFER OWNERSHIP AND/OR MANAGEMENT TO FAMILY OR CLOSE FRIENDS

The transfer of ownership and/or management to family or close friends is routinely the exit strategy of choice for an entrepreneur who establishes a family business or who has a child, relative, or close family friend who is considered the heir apparent to the business. At first glance, it might seem like transferring your business to a relative or friend would be a straightforward exit strategy. However, when you take a closer look, you realize that there is a great deal of planning, training, and assessment that goes into this type of exit strategy. This is especially true because the succession exit strategy involves two components: (1) the transfer of control of the day-to-day business operation to a person (or people) that you select to succeed you, and (2) the transfer of assets in the business to a person (or people) that you select. The reality is that the person (or people) to whom you transfer power may not be the same person (or people) to whom you transfer the business' assets. As a result, it is essential that you work closely with reputable professionals such as a tax specialist, an estate planner, and an attorney. These experts will be the most knowledgeable in helping you to not only avoid dangers, but also maximize the benefits associated with transferring power, management, and assets over to family members and/or friends.

Although you will require the assistance of qualified professionals, there are certain steps that you may take on your own, including:

- Identifying a successor that is not only highly trainable and motivated, but also interested in being committed to the business.

- Determining the transition time.

- Creating a transition timeline, including goals and tasks that must be accomplished leading up to the assigned transition date.

- Developing a successor-training schedule, including business-operating and growth-strategy competencies that must be achieved.

- Discussing your role — if any — in the business post transfer.

If you want to ensure that there is a smooth transition associated with transferring the power and assets of your business to a person (or people) you select, then you must plan for it. Otherwise, your heirs will likely pay the price for your failure to map out the best possible scenario. This may seem farfetched when you do not have money to start a business. However, even without money, you can begin by researching and asking questions that play a part in helping you make good business decisions from the start.

## SELL TO EMPLOYEES/PARTNERS

For some entrepreneurs, it may make sense to exit by selling the business to employees and/or partners. This strategy is popular for a number of reasons, including: (1) employees and/or partners are knowledgeable about the business and have an interest in ensuring that the business not only succeeds, but also grows; (2) this exit strategy allows for a smoother and quicker transition from the business to whatever you decide to do next; (3) it resolves the issues associated with scheduling meeting and tours with potential third-party buyers who want to evaluate your business and review your financial records; and (4) it can be executed gradually in order to prevent too much disruption to the business. As a result, selling to employees and/or partners has the potential to be a seamless transaction with little to no disruption in the daily operations. In addition, confidential information will remain private, and management may become invigorated and more focused on profitability.

Despite the advantages associated with selling a business to employees and/or partners, it is important that you plan early and re-evaluate often. As soon as possible you should:

- Identify a qualified employee and/or partner to buy your interest in the business. This should be someone who has the requisite skill sets, motivation, and funds to purchase the business.

- Determine if you or the business can feasibly finance a portion of or the entire purchase price in the event that you find the right employee or partner who has the desired skill sets and motivation, but lacks funds.

- Create comprehensive training modules that will help you assess whether an employee and/or partner possesses the necessary foresight and management skills to assume ownership and ensure long-term growth and profitability.

Prior to selling your business to an employee or partner, you should engage a reputable business transactions lawyer and tax specialist to help you draft agreements and determine the right course of action based on current tax laws and regulations.

# SELL TO A THIRD PARTY

Selling your business to a third-party outsider is another exit strategy. In this situation, timing is critical because you want to be in a position to sell your business not only when it is doing well, but also when there remains potential for growth. This will ensure that you can maximize your profit, take steps to minimize your tax liability, and retain leverage during contract and price negotiations. Typically, selling your business to a third party outsider will require you to:

1. Prepare

    - Create goals
    - Hire an experienced team
    - Perform due diligence

2. Market

    - Create a buyer qualification checklist
    - Showcase the business in a positive light
    - Secure a qualified buyer
    - Ensure buyer signs confidentiality agreement
    - Have buyer perform due diligence

3. Negotiate

    - Obtain a letter of intent
    - Perform final due diligence
    - Adhere to confidentiality agreement

4. Close

    - Sign the purchase agreement
    - Close the deal

Selling your business to a third-party outsider can present complicated issues. You want to be protected against potential lawsuits for alleged misconduct such as fraud or misrepresentation. It will be in your best interest to utilize the services of a seasoned business broker, investment banker, and business transactions lawyer to assist you with marketing, negotiations, documentation, and closing.

## GO PUBLIC
## (AN INITIAL PUBLIC OFFERING)

In an initial public offer (IPO), a private business will sell some of its stock to the public. When executed correctly, an IPO can be incredibly profitable. However, an IPO is typically an unrealistic exit strategy for a small business because of the enormous initial costs and commitment associated with the process.

There are considerable initial costs (millions and millions of dollars) associated with an IPO, including:

- Management team
- Underwriting
- Legal
- Accounting
- Printing
- Stock exchange list fees
- SEC filing fees

Moreover, the initial effort and commitment associated with going public are enormous, requiring tremendous focus from a strong, competent management team. The following are questions that must be answered in the affirmative before you embrace an IPO as your exit strategy:

1. Does the business have a management team and board of directors that are mentally, physically, financially, and personally equipped to transition into a public company?

2. Will the business' productivity, profitability, growth potential, and financial hygiene attract investors?

3. Is the business' brand strong, highly visible, and globally recognized?

4. Are future profits highly predictable?

5. Does the business have solid intellectual property positioning and key commercial agreements?

6. Does the business have a solid competitive advantage and position in relationship to its competitors?

7. Are current market conditions favorable for the business' industry?

8. Can the business withstand the initial and ongoing legal, accounting, and regulatory scrutiny and costs placed on public companies (including initial and ongoing filings and disclosure requirements, corporate control, and external and internal monitors and regulations over financial reporting)?

9. Can the business adhere to investor demands that hinge on establishing and maintaining good standing with other key participants in the capital markets (including stockholders, analysts, regulators, and the financial press)?

10. Does the business have the capability and flexibility to change its model or take actions that will need stockholder approval?

If you answered yes to all of these questions, then an IPO might be the right exit strategy for your business. Otherwise, you may want to consider a more cost and time-effective end goal for your business.

## ACQUISITION

An acquisition is an exit strategy that involves a business' shares and assets being purchased and taken over by another business that will be clearly recognized as the new owner. In short, the business that is purchased and taken over will cease to exist. Acquisition is not a do-it-yourself exit strategy. You will need a lawyer who specializes in mergers and acquisitions as well as business negotiations and a certified public accountant who is an expert regarding the tax implications associated with acquisitions.

Although the benefits of a well-executed acquisition include a potentially high valuation of a business that results in a high sale price as well as the ability to negotiate the price, acquisitions also tend to be messy and can fall apart at the last minute. An acquisition is completely dependent on attracting competitors that are interested in your products and/or services and are willing and able to buy your business.

The acquisition process for the seller is usually two pronged:

1. Groundwork

   - Perform and complete business analysis and due diligence
   - Prepare industry analysis, evaluating comparable businesses
   - Assess business positioning
   - Evaluate strategic options
   - Identify potential buyers
   - Agree on business valuation
   - Establish a business plan
   - Create financial predictions
   - Develop a sales presentation

2. Implementation

- Contact and qualify potential buyers
- Schedule and conduct preliminary and follow-up meetings with potential buyers
- Secure letters of intent
- Read and assess offers
- Ensure buy-in from employees, partners, and other stakeholders
- Choose a buyer
- Negotiate terms and conditions
- Consult with lawyer in preparation of final agreement and other relevant documentation
- Close the deal

It is also worth mentioning that an acquisition is usually not a quick or painless exit strategy; there will be contractually documented conditions associated with the acquisition, which may include an enforceable non-compete agreement as well as a requirement for you to maintain in management for a specified time during the transition period of takeover.


## DRAIN THE BUSINESS

Draining a business is probably the easiest exit strategy because it involves little planning and you can accomplish it with minimal professional consultation. This is an especially effective strategy for small to midsize businesses that are sole proprietorships. In order to drain the business prior to your exit, simply take as much money as you can out of the business on a yearly basis. You will only need to maintain enough cash in the business to ensure that it operates profitably. You can accomplish this by increasing your salary and giving yourself bonuses. In the end, if you have the means to settle your outstanding debts, then you are free to close the business and liquidate your assets. The only real drawback to this strategy is that with a larger salary comes greater tax liability.


## LIQUIDATE

Much like draining a business, liquidating a business is relatively straightforward. Liquidating involves converting the business' assets (furniture, fixtures, equipment, and inventory) to cash by selling them to a consumer. Liquidation is not a complicated process, but it also does not reap the greatest profits because there is often a sense of urgency to sell the assets, and thus, less leverage in terms of price negotiations. The biggest decision when liquidating your business is whether you will liquidate the business yourself or hire a liquidation professional. Whatever the case may be, you get to keep all the profits from the liquidation less the cash you will use to pay off the business' remaining debts.

# CHAPTER FOUR:
# GET THE BUSINESS OFF THE GROUND

*"THE GREATEST VIRTUE is not LOVE, but DISCIPLINE"*

When I started a business with no money 20 years ago, the technological advancements were nowhere near what they are today. The Internet had been developed. However, it was slow, sparse in terms of content and marketing platforms, and mostly inaccessible to the general public. As a result, I had to knock on doors, visit churches, and meet with community leaders in an effort to get my business off the ground, letting the community and potential clients know that I had arrived and built a business that offered a valuable service. My marketing efforts required consistency, discipline, and drive—not money —in order for them to pay off. It was my goal to sit on as many sofas and pews as possible in my target area. I accomplished my goals, and my efforts paid off in the form of sales and profits. When I first opened my doors for business, there were people lined up around my office building waiting to be served.

I still recommend that you knock on doors, visit religious organizations, and meet with community leaders in order to get your business off the ground. However, today there are also many other opportunities for marketing your business with no money. Some of these opportunities are available via the Internet in the form of website platforms for activities such as blogging, networking, messaging, and uploading videos/images. If you live in a major city or progressive town, then you do not even need to purchase a computer right away. You can easily visit a local public library and, in most instances, obtain a free library card. The library card will provide you with access to public computers that are linked to the Internet.

This chapter outlines effective marketing media that you can implement

—with no money—as long as you are willing and able to put in the time and effort required to develop content that speaks to your brand and meet with people to promote your products and/or services.

## DEVELOP A MARKETING STRATEGY

You should develop a marketing plan prior to implementing any type of marketing media. A marketing plan will help you organize your thoughts, maintain focus, articulate what products and/or services your brand offers, and define terms for measuring success. In the marketing plan you will answer the following questions:

- What are the company's current target market(s)?

- What are the company's future target market(s)?

- What are the company's marketing objectives? How will the company measure performance against the objectives?

- What is the timeframe for accomplishing the objectives?

- How does the company fit into the current marketplace?

- What role with respect to the marketing plan will each person assume?

- What are the relevant competitive forces that impact the company?

- What are the relevant economic forces that impact the company?

- What are the relevant legal and regulatory forces that impact the company?

- What technological forces impact the company?

- What sociocultural forces impact the company?

- What competitive advantages does the company have over the competition?

- What are the company's shortcomings with respect to implementing the marketing plan? How can they be overcome? How can they be transformed into strengths?

- What are some opportunities in the marketplace that can be exploited if addressed appropriately?

- What company strengths match opportunities in the marketplace?

- What are the obstacles, threats, or barriers that may hinder the successful implementation of the marketing plan?

- What product and/service attributes will be highlighted?

- What marketing media will be utilized? Who will be responsible for implementing and overseeing the execution of these marketing pursuits in a timely and effective manner?

When you have answered the questions, you will have the information you need to draft a marketing plan. The following outline may help you arrange your marketing plan. Do not feel constrained by the format because the content is what matters the most.

## Executive Summary

The executive summary is the overview of the marketing plan

and the methods for meeting those objectives. It should also point out the lack of a budget and how performance will be measured. Even though the executive summary is at the beginning, it may be beneficial to write it after the rest of the plan is formulated.

## Business Overview

The business overview lists and explains the products and/or services that your business will market to consumers/clients. The business overview should include an analysis of what makes your products and/or services different from what is currently offered in the marketplace. This is where you would examine your business' strengths, weaknesses, opportunities, and threats.

## Target Market

The target market component of the plan specifies your target market in terms of potential customers and the geographic location to be served. Include as much demographic information as possible (e.g. income, age, and gender).

Also, determine the number of people in your geographic area that actually match your business' target market profile and, if it is possible, divide your target market into significant categories. This will allow you to customize your marketing messages to speak to each group's needs and/or desires.

## Marketing Objectives

The marketing objective will include your sales and market objective over a specified timeframe.

## Marketing Strategies

Marketing strategies will delineate your strategies for

product/service mix, pricing, promotion, place/area, and positioning:

- Product/Service Strategy – Include the mix of products and services you will sell, how the mix will best meet customer needs, and how it compares to your competitors' mix of products and services.

- Pricing Strategy – Communicate your prices for your products/services and how they compare to competitors' prices. Address the impact the pricing will have on your level of sales.

- Place/Location Strategy – Convey whether the location of your business best meets the needs of your customers and/or establishes a competitive edge.

- Promotional Strategy – Discuss the promotions that your business will implement and how they will increase customer awareness and incentivize customers to buy your products and/services.

- Positioning Strategy – Describe the values you want customers to associate with your business and how they distinguish you from competitors.

## Execution Tasks

Execution tasks should list the activities needed to carry out each marketing strategy. Include a description of each task, the name of a person responsible for its completion, and a target date for completion. Establishing an action plan ensures clarity and accountability.

You might find it helpful to include a table:

| Task | TASK DESCRIPTION | PERSON ASSIGNED | COMPLETION DEADLINE | DATE COMPLETED |
| --- | --- | --- | --- | --- |
|  |  |  |  |  |
|  |  |  |  |  |
|  |  |  |  |  |
|  |  |  |  |  |
|  |  |  |  |  |

## Sales Forecasts

Sales forecasts should include a prediction of the sales revenue you expect as a result of the implementation of the marketing plan. Provide an explanation of the assumptions on which the sales forecast is based, including how it connects to the number of potential customers in the target market.

## Evaluation of Results

The evaluation of results section should describe what criteria will be used to define success for the plan, and how success will be measured. It is important to monitor success on a consistent basis in an effort to determine what strategies are working, when they are working, and on whom they are working.

Once the plan is established and implemented, take care to ensure that the plan is being followed. Address deviations from the plan by either updating the plan to reflect the changes or minimizing them as much as possible.

You may consider adding some of the following "no money required" marketing approaches to your marketing plan:

- Network with Community Leaders

- Commit to Community Outreach

- Seek Publicity

- Utilize Social Media and Networking Platforms

- Place Ads on Free Websites

- Create Business Alliances (Cross-Promotional Marketing)

- Become an Expert

Of course, these are just a small sampling of the many opportunities that exist today. On an ongoing basis, talk to other entrepreneurs about their marketing efforts and the no-cost/low-cost platforms they use. You will be amazed at the response.

## NETWORK WITH COMMUNITY LEADERS

Networking with community leaders is an effective way to build brand awareness and loyalty in your community. Most community leaders welcome and encourage entrepreneurs to meet with them. This is especially true if your business intends to be a good neighbor and possibly contribute to community development plans that are either in the works or already underway.

Your first meeting with a community leader can be a brief (5 to 10 minutes) introduction to you, your business, and your goals as they pertain to the business. Call ahead to schedule a meeting instead of just dropping by an office unannounced. This ensures that you are maximizing your time and effort. After the initial meeting, schedule another meeting. Any meeting that you have should have a specific purpose in mind. That purpose should be to obtain contact information for other community leaders that may be in a position to either get the word out about your business or connect you with other leaders who can.

During a meeting with a community leader, you can:

- Discuss your business and industry in a confident and knowledgeable manner. Assert yourself as an expert in your industry.

- ➤ Describe how you package and price your products and services.

- ➤ Express the value you bring to customers.

- ➤ Communicate the company's identity, brand, and culture.

- ➤ Tell how your business differs from the competition.

- ➤ Talk about where the industry is heading from the standpoint of technology and finances.

- If applicable, delineate your plan to create jobs for which people in the community would qualify.

- Ask about current and future community development plans as well as any potential financial incentives for businesses to build and stay in the community.

Maintain a high level of professional integrity in meeting with community leaders. Avoid conversations that become too personal or political. You do not want to alienate a potential resource within the community you serve.

## COMMIT TO COMMUNITY OUTREACH

Community outreach is an excellent marketing method for businesses when carried out correctly. This is especially true for local community businesses that will rely on a local customer base for sales. Community outreach is the ultimate win-win situation. The community wins because your business gives back to the community it serves. At the same time, your business wins because it benefits from positive exposure and greater visibility of its products and services, which translates into increased sales and profitability for your business.

In the event that you decide to incorporate community outreach into your marketing plan, then I highly recommend that you adhere to the following guidelines:

- Ensure that your community outreach efforts and initiatives are in line with your business' vision, mission, values, culture, and target markets. For example, if you operate a pet grooming business, then you might want to sponsor or volunteer to organize an adoption event with a local animal shelter.

- Ensure that you tell as many people as possible about your community outreach experiences. Post the story (make it interesting!) along with plenty of pictures and, if possible, a short video on all social media outlets, including, but not limited to Facebook, Twitter, Pinterest, Tumblr, YouTube, LinkedIn and relevant blog posts. Also, create press releases and submit them to your local news outlets.

- Ensure that you track responses and sales revenue that are a direct result of your community outreach efforts.

## SEEK PUBLICITY

Publicity is free and effective. It is newsworthy information that attracts attention or garners support. Often, it is a ringing endorsement from a third-party media outlet. It is wonderful when the publicity is illustrating your business in a positive light. However, publicity—in most cases—does not happen on accident. It is the result of a well thought out PR campaign. In order to achieve your marketing objectives through publicity, take the following steps:

- **Specify your target media in your area**

  - Online and print newspapers
  - Television
  - Radio programs

- **Identify who you should contact regarding your industry**

  - Contact the reporter or producer directly (often times this contact information can be obtained from the Internet)
  - Develop your own media directory, include names, addresses, telephone numbers, and email addresses

- **Develop story angles**

  - Ensure that your story has a narrow focus (it may help to present a question that you will answer in your story)
  - Ensure the stories are appropriate for the media outlet you approach
  - Ensure that your story is new and interesting

- **Make the pitch**

  - Document your ideas and submit them to a reporter or producer in a letter
  - Keep it short – no more than 250 words

- **Follow up**

  - Follow up with a phone call within a week of submitting the letter
  - If additional information is requested, send it immediately

You might also consider submitting frequent press releases to www.PRLog.com. PRLog.com is a free press release distribution service that circulates your press releases over the Internet. Again, make sure it is interesting and newsworthy before submitting. This will increase its chances of being released to the public.


## UTILIZE SOCIAL MEDIA AND NETWORKING PLATFORMS

Without question, every business should take advantage of the benefits associated with marketing on social media platforms and networking websites. As soon as possible you should establish and maintain an active profile for your business on Facebook, Twitter, Tumblr, Pinterest, and Instagram. You may post images, videos, special offers, upcoming events and promotions, community outreach activities, and other useful information on these platforms.

It is important that you map out a strategy for adding quality content to social networking websites. Keep in mind that you will be engaging directly with your customers on these outlets, so it will not be enough just to throw up pictures and captions. Your posts should be purposeful and interesting, keeping in mind your business' target market and overall marketing objectives.

Also, remain mindful that social media and networking platforms are actually a form of word-of-mouth advertising. Therefore, be careful to ensure that the wording of content and the images that you post accurately represent your brand. If necessary, run everything through reliable filters—family, friends, and business associates—prior to making an official post. You do not want to add content that may potentially tarnish or harm your brand name. Your customer base may let down their guards and post comments and images that will provide you with valuable insight about your products and/or services or those of your competitors. However, you—as a business owner—should be deliberate and hyperconscious about what and when you post online.

You will find that the ongoing technological advancements in applications on social networking platforms will serve your business well when they are fully exploited. For example, Facebook's Page Insights tools and dashboard allow you to gather data related to interpersonal exchanges on your Fan Page. You can obtain data and develop metrics on Fan demographics that will help you customize messages and talking points.

## ADVERTISE ON FREE CLASSIFIED AD WEBSITES

There are numerous websites that allow businesses to post ads for free. Some of these websites include:

- [www.craigslist.org](www.craigslist.org)

- [www.kijiji.com](www.kijiji.com)

- [www.loot.com](www.loot.com)

- [www.backpage.com](www.backpage.com)

- [www.gumtree.com](www.gumtree.com)

- [www.oodle.com](www.oodle.com)

- [www.local.com](www.local.com)

- [www.usfreeads.com](www.usfreeads.com)

In order to advertise on classified ad websites, you must take the following steps:

1. Register on each website.

2. Develop an ad that is brief and purposeful (special offer, promotion, etc.).

3. Log into the site and copy and paste the content onto the site.

Take the time to become familiar with each ad site and its parameters. You may find that some ads must be posted several times on the same site in order to reach various regions.

## DEVELOP BUSINESS ALLIANCES (CROSS-

# PROMOTIONAL MARKETING)

In order to expand your customer base, consider developing business alliances with complementary, noncompetitive companies. For example, a dog trainer may team with a local pet store in an effort to promote each other. Each company provides the other marketing collateral to distribute to his or her customer base. In this way, each business gains access to the other's customer base via advertisements, brochures, flyers, references, and testimonials.

Do your homework prior to reaching out to a company in an effort to develop a cross-promotional relationship and strategy:

- Know your customer base (age, gender, income level, location, interests, etc.). Knowing your customer base will be essential in determining what complementary business shares a customer base with the same demographics.

- Research businesses in your area that target a comparable market. Make a list of the businesses prior to reaching out to them. You may want to visit the businesses several times and simply observe their customers prior to trying to develop a cross-promotional relationship with the business.

- Ensure that both sides will benefit from the cross-promotional arrangement. For example, the dog trainer may want to use the pet store's products in his business, whereas the pet storeowner may want to post signs around his store for the dog trainer.

## BECOME AN EXPERT

A guaranteed way to build brand awareness in your industry is to become an industry expert. In an effort to develop expert status, you may do the following:

- Establish a blog that focuses on industry-related topics

- Post comments on other blogs that focus on industry-related topics

- Write editorial pieces for industry-related magazines and journals

- Host webinars and seminars educating the public about your industry in general and your services specifically

- Reach out to producers in an effort to be a guest speaker on a radio show addressing topics related to your industry

Once you are an established expert in your industry, you have credibility with the public. This is a powerful position because you—as an expert—can impact behavior by making recommendations. Ultimately, your status as an expert will help your business increase sales and profitability.

# CHAPTER FIVE:
# WATCH THE CASH

*"In business, always mean what you say and say what you mean! Always be truthful. Never deceive anyone."*

Soon after I started my business without any money, the business not only began making money, it was profitable. I had more money than ever before. Nevertheless, throughout the entire time I operated my first business, I mismanaged the business' finances on a week-to-week basis, plugging holes and neglecting to set goals and make financial projections. More often than not, I placed my personal wants over my business' needs. These fiscally irresponsible practices proved detrimental to my ability to recover after the state unexpectedly shut down my business. This was an expensive and humiliating lesson to learn. I lost my home and other material possessions that I had acquired during the heyday of my first business. After losing my first business, I spent several years in a mental desert before I regained my will to move forward with a second business. The second time around would be different from the first. I learned to establish a monthly budget, set goals, and make projections.

As a business owner, you must implement best practices for managing money, including:

- Developing a monthly budget

- Evaluating fixed and variable expenses on a monthly basis

- Establishing aneEffective pricing structure

- Working with a reputable factoring company

- Working with a local bank

- Monitoring customer payment collections

- Prioritizing competing interests

By implementing best practices as they relate to financial issues, you become a more effective manager and reduce the risk of depleting all your money before meeting your business needs and obligations. You will make projections and then gather and analyze data to determine whether you are meeting/exceeding your sales goals. This process of gathering and analyzing data should keep you grounded in reality and focused on reducing expenses/overhead and improving profitability.

## DEVELOP A MONTHLY BUDGET

Do not overthink the development of a monthly budget. You should approach the development of a budget in the same way you might write out a recipe or directions to your favorite theater. Much like a recipe or directions, the monthly budget is a roadmap—a useful instrument—to ensure that your business reaches its financial goals. In order to develop the roadmap, you really only need the mathematical ability of a third grader. If you can add and subtract decimals, then you can create a budget. This is great news because it means that you do not need expensive budgeting software for your small business. You only need paper, pencil, and your brain.

### Step One

When you develop your monthly budget, I strongly suggest that you list your expenses—fixed and variable—first. You may find it easier to initially delineate your fixed expenses and then provide a best estimate for the variable expenses. All estimates should be realistic. Do not budget $25.00 a month for your electricity bill when you know that, on average, it is about $100.00 a month. Of course, if you invest in energy saving measures that should cut your energy costs by 75%, then you may be able to safely predict that your electricity bill will be reduced by $75.00 per month. Whatever the case may be, examine the facts when accounting for variable expenses. Business expenses typically include, but are not limited to the following:

- Estimated Taxes

  - Business
  - City/County
  - Payroll
  - Personal
  - Sales and use

- Licenses
- Dues
- Publications
- Mortgage/Rent
- Vehicle expenses

  - Fuel
  - Car payment
  - Maintenance
  - Repairs

- Insurance
- Utilities

  - Light
  - Heating
  - Water
  - Telephone
  - Internet
  - Trash removal

- Education
- Travel
- Meals
- Wages
- Employee benefit programs
- Uniforms or special clothing
- Office supplies, equipment, and stationery
- Legal services
- Accounting services
- Professional services
- Commissions and fees
- Printing
- Marketing and advertising
- Interest on business debt
- Postage and freight

In addition to listing fixed and variable expenses, it is highly recommended that you account for emergencies by setting aside a fixed amount of money each month. For example, you might want to budget $250.00 a month for emergencies and/or unforeseen expenses.

## Step Two

Add all of your business expenses in order to obtain the number that will reflect your total expenses for the month.

## Step Three

List your predicted income for the month.

## Step Four

Subtract the amount of your "Total Business Expenses" from your "Predicted Monthly Income." Document the difference. At this point, you will reach one of three conclusions: (1) there is more than enough money to meet your business' expenses; (2) there is just enough money to meet your business' expenses; or (3) there is not enough money to meet your business' expenses. In any event, the knowledge about your financial situation will empower you to make necessary decisions.

## Step Five

Make adjustments to your business' budget as necessary by evaluating expenses on a monthly basis to determine if there are opportunities to trim excessive spending. No expense should be deemed too large or too small to cut when it no longer benefits the operation and growth of your business. Along the same line, a monthly budget should not feel overly restrictive. If you determine that your business requires more dollars for marketing and advertising, then increase the amount for that expense and look for other expenses that you can either reduce or eliminate. By working to consolidate your expenses you will also help to reduce expenses and creditors.

## ESTABLISH AN EFFECTIVE PRICING STRUCTURE

Your products and/or services must be priced correctly if you expect your business to make money. There are several considerations that you must examine and resolve before establishing a pricing structure:

- Is there a demand for your product(s) and/or service(s)?

- What is the perceived value of your product(s) and/or service(s)?

- What can your target market afford to pay for your product(s) and/or service(s)?

- How does the quality of your service(s) and/or product(s) compare to those of your competition?

- What are your actual costs to produce and/or deliver your product(s) and/or service(s)?

- What environmental costs (taxes, regulations, labor cost, etc.) will impact the delivery of your product(s) and/or service(s)?

- Will your pricing structure maximize profits?

- Will your pricing structure help you secure market share?

- Will your pricing structure allow you to maintain price stability?

When you answer these questions, it is critical that you understand that your main objective is to gain market share. In most industries, the pie has already been sliced. Industry leaders possess the lion's share of the pie, leaving the crumbs for those businesses that lack innovation. Consequently, there are no slices left on the table. Your business' prices must give you a competitive advantage and position you to take slices of the market pie from other businesses.

In the event that you are running a business that is paid by the state or federal government, then prices may already be established by the government, leaving you with a "take it or leave it" proposition. Therefore, in order to compete in the public sector, you must track your operating expenses carefully to turn a profit and ensure that your expenses do not exceed your anticipated income.

## PAY YOURSELF A REASONABLE SALARY

Depending on how you structure your business, it may be legally mandated that you pay yourself a reasonable salary. Reasonable typically means the fair market value for your position as manager and/or CEO within your industry. However, not all business structures require this. So, in many instances it is left to the discretion of the business owners to place business needs ahead of personal desires.

As your business begins to make money, it may be tempting to use the business as your personal automated teller machine, taking money out the business whenever and for whatever you think you can purchase. Do not do it! This type of behavior signals a lack of discipline. Inevitably, the business expenses will go unpaid or underpaid. There may not be enough money to market or hire qualified people.

The best policy when running a growing a business is to live within your means. This means that in addition to creating a budget for your business, you should create a personal budget to map out your personal expenses and plan major personal purchases.

## WORK WITH A REPUTABLE FACTORING COMPANY

In the event that you do not qualify for bank financing and you prefer not to absorb the costs associated with meeting the expectations of an equity investor, then you may find it beneficial to work with a reputable factoring company as you begin to build your business. I did not know about factoring companies when I started my first business with no money. However, once I discovered the advantages associated with working with a reputable factoring company, I utilized one on a temporary basis to increase cash flow while I grew the second business I started with no money.

### What is a Factoring Company?

A factoring company is a third-party firm (or factor) that purchases a business' accounts receivable and, in exchange, provides the business with a cash advance that is leveraged against that anticipated revenue. As a result, a factoring company does not make loans. This works to your advantage if you have large accounts receivable and customers with good credit ratings.

As the owner of the accounts receivable, the factoring company collects the owed receivables. This is just one of the reasons why receivable factoring is more expensive for businesses to improve cash flow rather than traditional bank financing. If you decide to work with a factoring company, then you should compare rates and work with a factoring company that has a longstanding reputation for integrity and fair business practices. Obtain answers to the following questions before entering into an agreement with a factoring company:

- What fees does the factoring company charge? Are the charges flat or a percentage of the total accounts receivable value? Are there additional fees associated with costs of conducting business?

- What are the factoring company's terms?

  - Understanding the factoring company's terms can potentially help you negotiate more favorable terms for your business.
  - A contract with a factoring company is usually a one-year agreement that will automatically continue for another year unless you provide a notice in the manner specified by the agreement.

- Does the factoring company offer recourse and non-recourse factoring?

  - Recourse factoring means that you are legally responsible in the event that the factoring company cannot collect on your customer invoices. Typically, recourse factoring is less expensive than non-recourse factoring.
  - Non-recourse factoring means that the factoring company assumes all the risks associated with collecting on your customer invoices.
  - It is to your advantage to work with a factoring company that offers both recourse and non-recourse factoring. This is essential when some of your customers are more likely than others to default on their payments.

- How long has the factoring company been in business?

  - Extensive experience in the factoring industry is desirable.

- Does the factoring company have enough capital to grow with your business?

  - You may be able to determine whether a factoring company has enough capital to grow with you by finding out the factoring company's typical account size, the factoring volume of the factoring company's biggest client, and whether the company has a limit on the number of debtors it can acquire.

- What services beyond financing and collections does the factoring company offer?

  ➢ Additional factoring services may include providing customer credit information and competitor evaluations. These services can help you make informed business decisions as your business grows.

## WORK WITH A LOCAL COMMUNITY BANK

Large commercial banks are not in business to help small businesses grow. They are designed to take your money. Find a local community bank that knows you and wants your business to succeed. The advantages to working with a local community bank over a large commercial bank often include:

- Lower fees
- Better interest rates
- Better terms on credit cards and loans
- Greater likelihood of securing a small business loan
- Shared interest in the advancement of the community in which your business operates

## MONITOR CUSTOMER PAYMENT COLLECTIONS

If at all possible, avoid the labor and headaches associated with customer collections by requiring your customers to pay in full in advance of them receiving your business' product(s) and/or service(s). However, when a prepay payment structure is not practical, feasible, and/or widely accepted in your industry, then it will be necessary for you to be vigilant with respect to ensuring that your customers pay your business what it is owed.

I do not recommend that you maintain your accounts receivable books manually unless you are only working with a few clients. Instead, utilize accounting software that will allow you to generate reports that identify delinquent customers, the amount that they owe, and how far behind they are with making their account current.

Once you have an accounts receivable monitoring and tracking system in place, then you can develop in-house collection procedures. Some businesses will send reminder letters with information on how the customer can take immediate action to rectify the matter and make his or her account current. Other businesses will discontinue ongoing services until the account no longer has an outstanding balance.

No matter what collection systems and procedures your business adopts, they will only be effective when they are consistently implemented and enforced. Otherwise, you will discover that you spend more time recording losses than earning profits.


## PRIORITIZE COMPETING INTERESTS

As a business owner, there may come a time when you do not have enough money to cover all of your monthly expenses. In a situation like this, you must prioritize the expenses that are essential to the survival of your business. In my experience, the first priorities are rent, utilities, payroll, and taxes. Also, during economic downturns and other stressful economic times, it will be important to continue an aggressive marketing campaign that will drive business and turn profits. For all other expenses:

- Reach out to creditors in an effort to establish more favorable payment arrangements.

- Eliminate expenses that are not vital to the survival of your business.

Most importantly, remain faithful. Do not fear lawsuits or creditors. Remain focused on the survival of your business. You can settle lawsuits when you are making money.

# CHAPTER SIX:
# ADAPT OR PERISH

*"Being in business for yourself can be an extremely LONELY ROAD! But remember, there is always one helping hand you can call on when everybody else WILL LEAVE YOU! Keep your eyes on the PRIZE!"*

My first business perished because it could not adapt to the hostile environment in which it was ultimately situated. For a number of years, my business basked and prospered in an environment that was not only friendly, but also supportive. As a young, first-generation entrepreneur, I lacked the knowledge and discipline to develop an agile business. I ignored warning signs that should have provoked me to take action and prepare my business for change. Instead, I chose to focus on personal interests that had nothing to do with ensuring the survival of my business. Complacency took root in my business and manifested its presence as a plague. The business' systems moved along day by day in a robotic fashion. Everyone was comfortable in his or her role within the company because paychecks were seemingly reliable. Nevertheless, the business was ill-suited for evolution. It was a one-trick pony that relied exclusively on a Medicaid-funded program that hung in the balance from one election cycle to the next. It was doomed to face extinction because there was no strategy in place to give it a chance to continue.

Now I have the opportunity to share the lessons that I have learned regarding the importance of weaving agility into the fabric of your business. When consistently implemented, these lessons increase the likelihood that your business will remain after others have ceased to exist because of their inability to adapt. In order to increase your flexibility and relevance in an ever-changing business environment, you must (1) heed and act upon warning signs, (2) ask more questions, (3) embrace change, (4) read with a focus on growth and survival, (5) work toward innovation, and (6) diversify your product and/or service offerings.

## HEED AND ACT UPON WARNINGS SIGNS

In order to survive in business, you must heed and act upon warning signs quickly, aggressively, and on an ongoing basis. Warning signs may reach you in the form of whispers, rumblings, and/or roars. Train yourself to hear the whispers in the industry about new technological advances, rumblings regarding trends that are gaining traction in the marketplace, and roars of economic upheaval. Otherwise, by the time you begin to notice the changes, your business will already be on the path to extinction. In order to heed and take action when various outlets and individuals sound a warning, you must have an acute awareness of the current business environment at all times.

### Know Your Position

To begin, you should recognize your current position in the environment, noting that your position should always be changing for the better. Answer these key questions in an effort to determine your business' present identity in your industry's larger ecosystem:

- What market share do I possess in the segment of my industry? How does that compare with the market share currently owned by my competition?

- Who is the recognized leader in my industry? If I am not the leader, how do I compare to the leader with respect to business model, systems, and product and/or service offerings?

- What advancements can I institute that allow me to gain greater market share in my industry?

## Recognize Threats and Potential Threats

Once you understand your position in the current business environment, the next step is to identity threats and potential threats to your business' survival. These threats and potential threats exist within your business, your industry, and the universe. Consequently, leave no stone unturned when seeking out threats and potential threats to your business.

Threats and potential threats to the survival of your business include, but are not limited to:

- Complacent business owner
- Rogue employees
- Dissatisfied customers
- Outdated technology
- Ineffective business systems
- Obsolete business model
- New competitors and innovators a/k/a game changers
- Irrelevant product and/or service offerings
- Changes in customer preferences
- New economic factors that impact customer behavior
- New social factors that impact customer behavior
- New cultural factors that impact customer behavior
- New, modified, or repealed policies, laws, and/or regulations
- New political figures and/or agendas

## Develop Strategies Against Threats and Potential Threats

Once you know your position in the current business environment and have identified threats and potential threats to your business, then you are better informed regarding your strengths and vulnerabilities. At this point, you are equipped to develop strategies that will reinforce your strengths as well as eliminate or reduce your vulnerabilities. Your strategic approach should be holistic and realistic insofar as it takes into account every aspect of your business and can be implemented quickly, but also allows room for instituting necessary adjustments.

Some businesses choose to focus on marketing/sales or technology when developing a strategic approach for dealing with threats and potential threats, leaving other aspects of the business like operating procedures, operating expenses, human resources, and the overall business model unexamined. This partial strategy approach will only increase the risk of your business' demise due to your failure to adapt.


## ASK MORE QUESTIONS

Business owners and entrepreneurs who neglect to ask questions regarding the motivation behind and validity of their day-to-day decision-making are doing their businesses a great disservice. This lack of inquiry and curiosity can result in a business becoming inflexible and unwilling to change, even when its survival is at stake.

On the other hand, leaders who nurture a business culture that rewards people who challenge existing and/or anticipated policies, procedures, plans, and systems in a constructive and productive manner usually have healthy, agile businesses. It is not surprising that these are also the businesses where the most innovative people want to work.

Ask more questions because you may discover that you are trapped in a business mindset that belongs to a bygone era. As 21$^{st}$-century technological, social, and cultural advancements have paved the way for more efficient systems and business models, you may find that your business model and systems reflect practices that were cutting edge during the early part of the last century. Certainly, we can name trailblazers and once-upon-a-time industry giants that fell prey to this mentality. However, it is more important to recognize the perils of not asking meaningful questions regarding your business decisions early and often.

Leaders should ask and answer the following questions everyday:

- How has the market/industry changed during the past 24 hours?

- What is working within my business? Why is it working?

- What aspects of my business have fallen behind market/industry standards? How can these be improved?

- What has my business accomplished during the past 24 hours?

- What lessons have I learned during the past 24 hours that will benefit my business?

- What are my motives for remaining in this business?

- Have I reached any of my business goals today?

- Did I empower my team today?

- What challenges did I face today?

- What responsibilities did I delegate and/or reassign?

## EMBRACE CHANGE

Although the force of change presents challenges for businesses, it also creates new opportunities for growth. Therefore, change is good. The only thing that makes change a dangerous proposition is a lack of preparedness. Embrace change by preparing your business for it.

You prepare your business for change by asserting that no person, policy, procedure, plan, or program in your business is immune from being modified or eliminated. These components only exist within the business to safeguard the survival of the business. When certain components are identified as threats or potential threats to the business, then they must be addressed in order to preserve the business' sustainability.

Some entrepreneurs cite loyalty as a reason for not terminating ineffective employees or continuing to work with vendors that provide subpar goods and/or services. They place personal relationships ahead of taking appropriate actions that are in the best interest of their businesses. This type of rigid behavior breeds developmental stagnation in the business world. As a result, you should always weigh the outcome of maintaining threats and potential threats against the benefits associated with eliminating them.

You should also embrace change by learning how to utilize and navigate new technology and marketing platforms. This knowledge will guarantee your business' ability to reach existing and new customers with messaging and information regarding your products and services. If you still insist on only utilizing print advertising and fail to understand and utilize Facebook, Twitter, or YouTube, then you are preparing your business for burial in a grave.

It does not matter if change happens all at once or a little bit at a time; either way, it is certain to arrive.


## READ WITH A FOCUS ON GROWTH AND SURVIVAL

Read as though your business' life depended on it. Read books, newspapers, magazines, blogs, etc. Although it will be essential for you to read publications that focus on your business' industry, you will also benefit from reading publications offering a global perspective. However, you will not read just for the sake of entertainment; you will read in an effort to make connections between what is documented in the text, talked about in various media outlets and platforms, and identified as areas that need improvement in your business. How does the information speak to your business? That will always be the fundamental question.

Set aside time in your day to read. You might start by blocking an hour each day to read. As a practice, incorporate reading into your downtime. Consider reading when you are eating a meal, working out, waiting to board a plane, riding in a taxi, etc. While you are reading, log the date, time, name of publication, along with relevant findings into a small notebook. The notebook will serve as a reference tool. Your documented findings should include information about technological advancements, new lingo, names of up-and-coming players in your industry, policies, laws, and regulations that are in the pipeline, as well as opportunities.

After you have logged your findings into your reference notebook, you or someone you designate may want to perform additional research on a particular topic in an effort to gather more intelligence that may influence your business decisions. Use the information as a way to introduce new industry facts to your teams for the purpose of discussion. By analyzing such newly discovered information during your decision-making process, you reduce the risk of being caught unaware of any changes occurring in your business environment. Remember, the objective is to implement strategic plans that will allow your business to bend and sway—as opposed to break—under the pressures associated with change.

## WORK TOWARD INNOVATION

Position your business as an agent of change. This means that your business model is designed to upset the status quo, changing the rules of the game within your market and industry. Working toward innovation requires a business leader to undertake an unyielding quest to discover and/or develop simple, creative, and profitable solutions to consumer demands. In an effort to work toward innovation, you must recognize a problem, develop a purpose, and implement a prototype.

### The Problem

The first step in working toward innovation is to identify well-defined areas in your industry that are ineffective due to changes in technology, culture, social norms, etc. It is the square peg that your industry forces into the round hole. Typically, no one else in the industry will view it as a problem. Often, it is an overlooked nuance in the process or the application of a product that was intended for something else. Whatever the case may be, other businesses are content to "go with the flow" despite the fact that there may be a more effective solution waiting to be implemented.

### The Purpose

The second step in working toward innovation is to develop a purpose that is built around serving others and performing good will. If your only purpose is to make money, then your scope will be too narrow. You want your purpose to benefit and inspire as many people as possible. A purpose that is driven by serving others will compel you to look outside of your four walls for solutions. Not only will you talk to your customers, but you will also travel the globe to meet and talk with others who are pondering and/or tackling the same problems. You will have an opportunity to discuss your ideas and the ideas of others.

## The Prototype

The final step in working toward innovation is to develop and test a prototype. This step may take years to vet and perfect. However, all of the whispering, rumbling, and roaring in the various business media outlets, as well as the content in various publications, will be about you and the game changer that your business is developing. Businesses in the industry will change their business models, marketing plans, procedures, policies, and product/service offerings in an effort to adapt and survive the inevitable force that your business created.

## DIVERSIFY YOUR PRODUCT AND/OR SERVICE OFFERINGS

If you do not possess the drive or inclination to work toward innovation, then you must continually look for ways to diversify your product and/or service offerings. By diversifying your product and/or service offerings, you increase the likelihood that your business will remain relevant throughout time.

I can use my business as an example of maximizing opportunities to diversify service offering. My business, A Caring Home Care Services, is in the private-pay, non-medical, home healthcare industry. Initially, my service offerings included the following non-medical services:

- Adult care
- Elderly care
- Expectant mother care
- Alzheimer's care
- Bathing
- Dressing
- Companionship
- Monitoring
- Hospital sitting
- Medication reminders

- Post surgical care
- Short-term childcare
- Walking assistance
- Pet care
- Plant care
- Shopping and running errands
- Light housekeeping and laundry
- Meal preparation

In a conscience effort to expand my business' service offerings, become more competitive, and thus, increase my business' chances for survival, my business now offers the following additional, complementary services:

- Lawn care
- Home and apartment cleaning
- Handyman and remodeling

Your decision to diversify should be strategic. You may start by offering your newly added products and/or services to a sample group within your target market. Doing so will allow you to test the viability of the offerings as well as work out any kinks before executing a system-wide launch.

# CHAPTER SEVEN:
# GROW THE BUSINESS

*"In Business and Life, always do GOOD. By doing GOOD, your LIGHT will always shine in darkness."*

I was wiser when I started my current private-pay, non-medical homecare business, A Caring Home Care Services, than I was when I started my first business with no money. I was transformed by the love of God. I dedicated myself to a journey guided by faith, truth, self-awareness, self-discipline, and service. Along the way, I learned to treat people within my business organizations as partners by addressing their concerns and sharing the fruits of my business with them in the form of bonuses, pay increases, and a 401K plan. When I began to honor my employees for their efforts, their loyalty toward my business and me grew. Consequently, my business prospered and continues to prosper. It was this business growth that positioned me for franchising.

I always wanted my business to be fully engaged in the open market because of the limitations I endured within the public sector. Once I opened A Caring Home Care Services, I knew that I wanted to expand and give other people an opportunity build a bright future. By chance, I discovered franchising, a business expansion strategy. Franchising provided the platform I was seeking in order to grow my business and provide others with an opportunity to open, run, and grow their own businesses. In order to franchise, I learned that there were certain essential components I had to develop, including a franchise business plan, franchise legal documents, a marketing plan, sales strategy, and an operations manual. Once these documents were developed, I possessed the tools I needed to launch a franchise program. The rest was up to my team and me. Our mission was to sell franchises and support franchisees in an effort to ensure mutual success.

# WHAT IS FRANCHISING?

In order for a business expansion strategy to qualify as a franchise, the following three elements must be present:

1. A license

2. Continuous training and support

3. A fee and/or royalty

A franchise is an ongoing, contractual relationship in which a franchisor—the business entity that owns the franchise business system—provides a franchisee with the following:

- A license to utilize its (1) brand, (2) operating system, and (3) marketing and distribution system

### AND

- Continuous training and support in organizing, operating, merchandising, marketing, sales, managing, training, and hiring.

The franchisor provides the license and support to franchisees in exchange for a fee and/or royalty that the franchisee must pay to the franchisor.

In a franchise, franchisees are legally obligated to operate the franchise business system as prescribed by the franchisor. The franchisor establishes system-wide operating and marketing standards in an effort to maintain the integrity of its proven system as well as ensure brand consistency and stability.

Along the same line, the franchisor must be dedicated to building and nurturing a franchise network that places great urgency on: (1) customer growth, retention, and satisfaction; (2) market saturation; (3) concept adaptability; and (4) high profit margins.

A quality franchise system will meet the following qualifications:

- Profitable, including current franchisees
- Well organized
- Experienced franchise support team
- National and global adaptability
- Excellent public acceptance and awareness in current markets
- Highly distinctive from competitors
- Established, efficient financial controls
- Established, efficient franchise monitoring systems
- Outstanding credibility
- Reasonably priced
- Strong franchisor integrity and commitment
- Proven success throughout the marketplace and industry

## FRANCHISE BUSINESS PLAN

Once I decided that I would franchise my business, I had to develop a franchise business plan. Franchising was new to me at the time. Therefore, I hired a reputable franchise consulting company to help me develop the plan.

The franchise business plan must be constructed to achieve the following objectives:

- Document decisions relating to the overall franchise model including: support programs, training programs, marketing programs, supplier programs, royalties, fees, technology, duration, initial investment, and additional costs

- Identify the franchise support team, their professional backgrounds, and their role(s) within the franchise system

- Measure the potential consequences of the decisions by establishing a one-year, three-year, five-year, and ten-year projected franchisor cash flow model

- Examine funding needs and options

- Outline franchise market focus as well as sales goals and strategies

- Describe the ideal franchisee

- Delineate a franchise development schedule

- Evaluate comparable active franchise offerings in the market place, listing the following company information:

  - Name
  - Number of franchised units
  - Number of company-owned units
  - Total units
  - Year franchise established
  - Year first franchise unit established
  - Total investment
  - Franchise fee
  - Royalty
  - Advertising fee

A franchisor must craft a plan that will result in worthwhile profits and positive business achievements for not only the franchisor entity, but also franchisees. A properly planned and implemented franchising system—as outline in a franchise business plan—typically leads to success and financial gain.


## FRANCHISE LEGAL DOCUMENTS

### Franchise Agreement and Disclosure Documents

The franchisor-franchisee relationship is governed by the franchise agreement and its supporting documents. Given the significance of the franchise agreement and disclosure documents, it is highly recommended that you hire an experienced franchise attorney to draft these documents for you. Although not an all-inclusive list, the franchise agreement must effectively accomplish the following:

- Articulate the duties and obligations of the involved parties

- Address, in great detail, the services that the franchisor entity will provide the franchisee

- List the rights of the involved parties

- Discuss the specifics of the franchise relationship from its inception to its conclusion

- Protect the franchisor entity

- Delineate all franchisees' defaults, which may harm the franchise system, and their respective consequences, up to and including termination of the franchise license

Before a franchisee signs a franchise agreement, he or she should carefully read the franchisor's disclosure documents (FDDs) in order to be as informed as possible regarding that specific franchise opportunity, franchisor organization, and franchisor-franchisee relationship.

Currently, A franchisor is obligated by law to give its FDD to prospective franchisees at least 14 days before an agreement is signed or money is exchanged. Among other information, the FDD should include the following about the franchisor company, alerting a potential franchisee of any possible concerns:

- Overview of the history, ownership, and corporate structure of the franchisor

- Business and management experience of the franchise management team and/or executive team

- Litigation involving the franchisor and/or its principal

- Bankruptcy (franchisor company as well as any officer or director)

- Fees, costs, and royalties

- Products and services source restrictions

- Franchisee's contractual duties and obligations

- Franchisee financing options (if any)

- Franchisor training and support assistance provided to franchisee

- Franchisee territory (if applicable)

- List of trademarks and patents, copyrights, and proprietary information regarding the franchise (Caution: Trademarks should be registered and owned by the franchisor.)

- Franchisee's legal obligation to participate in the actual operation of the franchise business

- List of restrictions on what the franchisee can sell

- Summary of the terms of the franchise agreement as they relate to renewal of the franchise agreement, termination of the franchise agreement, transfer of the franchise to a third-party entity, and dispute resolution

- Financial performance representation on how much current franchisees are earning (although most franchisors elect not to include an earnings claim because of the many variables—labor, product price, rent, shipping costs, etc.—that impact earnings

- Chart that shows the number of franchises opened, transferred, and closed

- Franchisor's audited financial statements

- Contracts that you are required to sign and a receipt confirming you have received the FDD

## MARKETING PLAN

A franchisor should develop a solid marketing plan prior to implementing a franchise program. The marketing plan should define a set marketing budget and outline how you will allocate those dollars in order to obtain the greatest number of qualified leads. A marketing plan should include the following:

- A summary of the purpose of the marketing plan as it pertains to your franchisor company

- Detailed discussion of all goals, including: budget, sales goals, territorial goals, target markets, types of media, and a timetable for execution of the marketing plan

- Support for marketing plan decisions in the form of market surveys, statistics, professional experience, etc.

- Marketing pieces (including, but not limited to: email, brochures, television ads, press releases, radio spots, website content/search engine optimization, and blogs) that will be utilized in the implementation of the marketing plan

- List of dollar amounts as they relate to the creation of marketing materials and the use of those marketing materials within various platforms (television, radio, newspapers, trade publications, etc.)

- Methods that will be used to track the effectiveness of the marketing plan

It is important to note that all franchise marketing material must comply with pertinent state laws and administrative guidelines. To this end, work with your franchise lawyer to ensure all statements made in your marketing materials are verifiable and compliant with the law.

## SALES STRATEGY

After you establish a marketing plan, you must develop a marketing strategy for screening/qualifying leads, preparing a sales presentation, closing a deal/turning a qualified lead into a franchisee.

To date, my primary sales strategy has been to utilize the services of a franchise sales outsourcing firm. A franchise sales outsourcing firm will perform the following sales tasks:

- Provide franchise marketing guidance
- Perform initial lead intake
- Input and update lead information in database
- Distribute marketing materials
- Attend tradeshows
- Execute preliminary lead qualification
- Ensure disclosure
- Carry out "Discovery Day"
- Manage and prepare franchise documents
- Provide support before and after closing

The franchisor is responsible for marketing costs and has complete discretion with respect to accepting or rejecting a lead when working with a franchise sales outsourcing firm.

Typically, franchise sales outsourcing firms have a compensation structure that includes a monthly processing fee in addition to fees for every successful sale.

Still other franchise sales outsourcing firms seek to take a percentage of the royalty stream or equity in the franchisor organization. This is something that I would never even consider. I advise against this type of payment arrangement in all situations.

I also do not recommend working with a franchise sales broker. Franchise sales brokers or Lead Referral Networks (LRNs) perform one role: they provide pre-qualified leads to participating franchisors in return for a success fee. Franchise sales brokers represent many franchisors and thus, use their discretion when deciding which leads will be matched with a particular franchisor.

Although franchise sales brokers may add a certain level of credibility to your franchisor company, they are third-party representatives, so once the selling starts, the franchisor is left to his or her own devices in terms of selling and closing the deal. With this in mind, if you decide to work with a franchise sales broker, then view the broker as a lead generator and not an extension of your franchise sales efforts.

## OPERATIONS MANUAL

Every franchisor must develop a franchise operations manual. The operations manual provides step-by-step instructions for every aspect of the franchise system, including establishing the business, managing the business, providing services, marketing and advertising, sales procedures, hiring and training, as well as all daily operating procedures and polices.

Moreover, the operations manual will serve as a ruler, measuring whether franchisees are adhering to franchisor-established standards. You will also utilize the operation manual during training, demonstrating that the franchisee can rely on the operations manual as a reference tool. Keep in mind that procedures, guidelines, and policies in the operations manual should be consistent with the terms and conditions outlined in the franchise agreement

I have included the master table of contents for my business as a representation of the types of topics you must address and detail when drafting your business' operations manual.

Note: the following master table of contents does not address my business' lawn care, cleaning, and remodeling services because the policies and procedures for those services are housed in separate manuals. You will be compelled to diversify services in order to build value in your franchise system. I started with private-pay, non-medical homecare services and later branched out into complementary services like cleaning, lawn care, and home remodeling and repair. These services presented opportunities for my franchisees to maximize their earning potential while addressing their customers' needs.

# A CARING HOME CARE SERVICES
# FRANCHISE OPERATIONS MANUAL

## MASTER TABLE OF CONTENTS

## A. INTRODUCTION



## B. ESTABLISHING AN A CARING HOME CARE SERVICES BUSINESS

# C. PERSONNEL

# D. OFFICE PROCEDURES



# E. A CARING HOME CARE SERVICES NON-MEDICAL, IN-HOME CARE SERVICE PROCEDURES

# F. MARKETING AND ADVERTISING

# Paid Sex - The Gigolo

And again a year has passed in which I neither found a partner nor had a decent date. Surely it can't be that hard to find the right man? I look at my calendar and see that even the last sex was forever ago. Actually, I don't even want to consider it as real sex, because the guy was so bad that I just want to erase this experience from my memory.

I tried so hard back then. I shaved everywhere, applied my most expensive perfume, put on pretty lingerie and even made up and for what? The guy almost tore my underwear after he didn't even notice it, then pushed my head down so I could blow him and came in less than five minutes. He didn't tidy up either and there wasn't even wine or cocktails, only lukewarm beer from his balcony. No. No. I don't want another one of those. The next time I want to have sex, I want it to be stylish. I want to be taken out to an expensive restaurant, drink the best wine and then be seduced. I want him to spoil me nicely and then fuck me in all imaginable positions until I have to beg him to stop because I can't do it anymore. That's exactly how it should be.

With these thoughts I log myself into the dating app again. Maybe I can catch one of these gorgeous guys there, but when the first message pops up, all my hopes and dreams are dashed.

"Hey doll, you up for some fun tonight? Come over if you want. I'm ready for you," someone writes, and a picture to go with it. Yuck! It's a picture of a half-erect dick that you can barely see for all that hair. Let's get rid of it.

The next news items follow which unfortunately look similar. Since I probably won't find anything here I quickly log out, so no one will get the idea to send me a message.

I put my phone aside and turn on the TV instead, maybe something cheeky on TV will do the trick.

I zap through the channels and find nothing except advertisements and some stupid shows. I feel like watching a really cheesy love movie and search for it in the media library. I already know most of the titles, that's probably one of the big advantages of being single, you always get to choose the TV programs yourself.

I discover a film that has been newly added and I am curious. Woman in her 30s is fed up with love and books a gigolo. I decide to have a look.

92 minutes go by in which I laugh, cry and sigh. Against all expectations the film is wonderful and of course the two of them come together at the end and he stops sleeping with women for money. And although I don't necessarily want to meet a man this way, the film gives me an idea: A gigolo! A gigolo for me! I certainly don't lack money and if I can pay for a soothing massage, then I can pay for a nice evening with sex.

Immediately I dig out my mobile phone again and look for an offer. There are numerous sites for men looking for affordable ladies but for women the selection is rather tiny. Nevertheless I find what I am looking for and search through several men in my region.

One of them catches my eye: James, late 20, 6'3 tall, muscular, dark-brown hair, blue eyes and a great smile; as far as I can tell from the half-cut picture. I imagine he probably wants to be discreet because in "real" life he has another job, which speaks well for him. I also like his description, he likes to spoil women and make them feel special.

I want to feel special, that's what I want. It will cost me as much as the few days in a wellness hotel that I I wanted to treat myself to. Sex for me though, my way, this is better, I hope anyway.

I dial the indicated number and a friendly woman answers on the other end that makes the appointments. I give her my name, my credit card number and the desired date. I'm afraid I can't make it this weekend. But the next weekend, James is still available.

"More time for anticipation," says the woman with a laugh. I think she's right.  Even if I could do without it I'd like it to happen right now. I just don't want to settle for my second choice, I want it to be just right.

"And how will that work out?" I ask curiously after she has all my data.

"I'll be sending James a message right away with the appointment and her phone number. He'll get back to you as soon as he can to discuss it further."

"What do we have to talk about?" I ask.

"The place where he can pick you up, your preferences, your taboos, etc."

"Oh. Okay. I see."

"After all, we want everything to be perfect, don't we?"

"Yeah, right." I hang up and suddenly I'm really excited. So James is going to come up and talk to me.

I put my mobile phone next to me, only to pick it up again two seconds later. I set it to "loud" so that I can hear when he calls me.

But the phone doesn't ring, not even the next day. He doesn't call until three days later, which is four days before the date. In the meantime I had given up on receiving a call from anymore, so I answer a bit confused when I see the unsaved number on the display.

"Hello?" I ask uncertainly.

"Hey, it's James. We have a date for Saturday night. I wanted to get in touch with you beforehand so that I could prepare everything perfectly," he says in a stunningly deep voice that immediately gives me goose bumps. I suddenly get nervous as I think about the man of my dreams sitting on the other end of the line.

"Yes, right," I say shyly, waiting for questions I can answer.

"Of course, I've already thought about a few restaurants, but I wasn't quite sure which one was right for you. Which cuisine do you like? Japanese? Italian or something completely different?"

"I like Japanese quite a bit, Italian as well," I answer quietly.

"Well, let me surprise you. Would you prefer red or white wine?"

"White wine."

"Wonderful! Can you speak freely now? You sound so quiet and silent. If you don't like it right now, I can call back," he says and I try to pull myself together. I'm sitting all alone in my apartment right now. Of course I can talk openly, but he already intimidates me a bit.

"No, I'm home and can talk freely," I now answer a bit more confidently.

"Good, then we'll move on to the delicate part. What are your preferences?"

I sit there thinking. It's never been easy for me to talk about something like this, but only those who speak up can be helped, so I tell him directly.

"I like it when I'm seduced slowly, that can start early at dinner, for example. Seduction for me shouldn't happen bluntly, as if a switch is suddenly flipped, it should build up a certain tension. I like to be spoiled. I like to kiss passionately with the tongue and fingers and then, when I am really horny, I like it to be harder. I like to be taken harder in all kinds of positions, in all kinds of places."

"Mhh ... that sounds just like my taste," he answers and I breathe a sigh of relief. "What do you dislike?"

I think again and again about the sex from last time. I tell him about this experience and he laughs.

"Don't worry, you won't experience that with me," he says.

Afterwards, I give him my address and we say goodbye.

When I hang up I notice how fast my heart beats. I am nervous and excited, and I'm really happy.

The rest of the week flies by. I am in a good mood and so relaxed at work that my colleagues even ask what's going on. Of course, I can't tell them about the fact that I'm going to pay a man for sex on the weekend, so I make up something.

And then finally it's time. It's Saturday and I take the liberty of sleeping in till noon. Then I do the weekly shopping, clean up and do the cleaning before I start to prepare myself in the early evening.

Like last time, I shave thoroughly, set out my best lingerie, wear make-up and perfume and choose my favorite dress. It's black and goes just above my knee, not only with a nice waist but a great décolleté and a crisp bottom too.

I look at myself in the mirror and feel sexy. I wave my hair carefully and slip into my new high heels, which I bought especially for the occasion.

And then the doorbell rings, he's right on time, right on time.

I quickly pack my bag and run downstairs. He stands at the entrance of the house and smiles at me.
Wow, what a man! He looks just like in the pictures and in my imagination, maybe even better.

"Hello! You look beautiful!" he says and spreads his arms to give me a kiss on the cheek on both sides as a greeting. He smells good and I notice how my legs start to shake. This always happens when I really like a man I have a date with.

He leads me to his car, opens the passenger door for me and waits until I'm seated to close it. He's a real gentleman.

Then he sits down next to me and again he beams at me.

"I know this really great new sushi restaurant, you'll love it," he says and then drives off. On the way there, he asks me about my job, my hobbies and my last holiday. There are no embarrassing breaks and great conversation continues in the same way at the restaurant. He is an attentive listener and seems very interested, I feel really comfortable.

We continue to chat as the foods on it's way. He laughs at my jokes and looks deeply into my eyes. When we are finished and my hand is on the table, he places mine in his and gazes at me from across the table.

"I can hardly wait until we get out of here and back to the hotel," he says as he runs his fingers over my hand. I immediately get goose bumps because it feels so good.

The waiter comes and asks if we want dessert. James looks at me, but I shake my head, I don't want to waste any more time here at the restaurant.

He leads me outside back to his car, but before he opens the door, he pushes me against the car. One hand on my waist, the other holding my face. He is so close that I can feel his hot breath. He comes even closer and our lips almost touch. He kisses me, first very gently and then more and more wildly. His left hand moves further down, grabs my bottom, kneads it and then presses me with it close to his crotch. I can feel his bump, which is getting harder and harder. My hands are on his back and shoulders, but before I can really cling to him, he lets go of me.

He smiles and then reaches past me to open the door.

Speechless I get in and sit down. I have not experienced such an intense kiss for a long time.

In silence we drive to the hotel. His hand he leads from time to time to my thigh. Very carefully he strokes it, while looking and smiling at me. I'm in 7th heaven!

We arrive and he takes out the key card from his pocket, he's already prepared everything. A bit nervous I walk beside him to the elevators. Unfortunately we are not alone. An older couple is standing with us in the elevator; otherwise I would surely have jumped on him or he on me.

The door opens and we get out. He quickly goes ahead to unlock the room door and then lets me in.

It's a nice room; modern, elegant, classic, just like him. He takes off my coat and bag goes to the fridge takes out a bottle of white wine. Pouring two glasses, he hands me one and we toast.

"Here's to a good time," he says and we both take a sip. No sooner have I put my glass down than he tears it out of my hand and puts it aside, grabs my face and kisses me. Stormy and passionate. Full of lust.

He pushes me backwards to the bed where I land. He kneels in front of me, pulls my high heels off my feet and strokes my feet before he continues on his way up. He kisses my entire body with his soft succulent lips.
30

He starts at the bottom and then works his way up until he reaches between my legs. Carefully he caresses my tender panties with his fingers. In the meantime my dress has pushed itself up by itself and without any effort it falls back on the spot. I enjoy his touch and kiss so much. But then he suddenly stops and appears again from between my legs. His face is suddenly right in front of mine. He looks at me and kisses me again before he pulls the dress all the way over my head. He admires me for a few seconds and then looks directly at me again.

"You are beautiful," he says, and kisses my neck.

This time he goes deeper. He reaches my shoulder, touches my chest and then my breasts. He pushes them out of my bra and sucks on my hard nipples with his soft lips first very gently and tenderly and then stronger and stronger.

After that it moves further down to my belly and finally gets back to my panties. He carefully pulls the lace from my hip then spreads my legs and holds my thighs with both hands.

I can feel his hot breath between my legs now. He comes closer and then I feel his warm, wet tongue against my pussy. With pleasure he licks once between my lips before he come to my clitoris. First gently and then more and more demanding he licks and sucks on her, stimulating me with the tip of his tongue again and again in my most sensitive spot.

A hand leaves my leg and suddenly I feel two fingers penetrating me. He pushes them in very deeply and then back as he finds my G-spot. He presses on her, stimulating her again and again and then leaves his fingers on my sensitive spot while his tongue continues to lick my clit.

I can feel my whole body contracting. My stomach and legs tense up, my head tickles and I know I'm about to come.

James continues patiently. He, too, realizes that it's almost my time. Again and again he runs his tongue over my clitoris, presses his fingers further deep into me and then I come loud and violently as I push my orgasm and squirt out. My hands are against my head and I breathe heavily. Wow! My whole body is shaking and I get dizzy.

James stops and leaves me for a moment to get my bearings. I see his face next to mine. He smiles at me, but doesn't say a word. He doesn't ask me the superfluous question of whether it was good or not, he can see it and does not need this confirmation.

For a few minutes we lie next to each other in silence until I feel his hand in my crotch again. He checks if I can go on and oh yeah, I am ready for his cock.

I stretch out my hand and pull on the fabric of his shirt. Before I can stand up to take it off him, he does it himself and presents me his perfectly defined body. My hands wander over his smooth skin and his muscles. Then they run across the waistband of his pants and I undo the belt and buttons. I pull down the zipper and pull his pants and his tight boxer shorts right down with me.

Excitedly I look at his cock, which jumps towards me. It is not only hard, but also big and thick, just the way I like it. Carefully I embrace it with my hand and go up and down once. Immediately he starts moaning, but then pushes me back onto the bed. He flings his pants off his legs and spreads mine again. He pulls his cock through my wet lips before he penetrates me with a firm push.

I'm moaning, he feels incredible inside me. He starts to fuck me slow and deep at first and then faster with every thrust. Again I feel the tingling in my body as he hits exactly the right spot to bring me to the climax again. He continues and then I come. I close my eyes, enjoy the warm feeling that flows through my body and the deep thrusts that I can now perceive even more intensely. This time he does not give me a break, but continues.

Now he turns me on my stomach and pulls me up by my hips. My butt protrudes towards him and he pulls close to him. I feel his cock again on my pussy and as he penetrates me in this position I can feel him even deeper as pushes even harder. I ravish in him as I claw my hands into the sheets and moan out in lust.

He moves again, this time pushing my bottom down as I lie flat on the bed and he pushes his beating dick into me. He keeps fucking me deep and hard and I hear him moaning as he's almost ready too.

Once more he pulls me toward him with my hip and then, with a few more pushes, he's brought to climax as well.

Breathing heavily, he lets himself fall beside me, looks for my gaze and smiles at me. He turns around and pulls me to him.

We lie next to each other for a while until I fall asleep, deeply.

When I wake up hours later, there's no sign of James, he's gone, but now without leaving me a message. "Thank you for a lovely evening. Breakfast is served at 8:00." I can't help smiling, I never thought I'd enjoy this so much, he and the agency knew exactly what I had in mind.

I turn over in bed once more, take a long bath afterwards and then go downstairs for breakfast before I drive home.

This was definitely more worthwhile than a stay in a wellness hotel.

# An Outdoor
# Adventure at the Lake

I t's a beautiful summer morning when I open my eyes and look out the window. There is not a single cloud in the sky and I get the urge to leave the house immediately and sit at the lake. Then I remember my date again. Hanno.

A couple of days ago I matched with him on Tinder and we wrote. He was actually quite detailed and suggested that we could do something together today. But I don't really feel like a date at a bar or a coffee shop. I want to ride a bike, go grocery shopping and stop at the lake to refresh myself in the cool water.

But why should a date keep me away? Who knows if tomorrow will still be as wonderful? I can always go to a cafe.

I write him that I would rather spend the day outside but somehow he misunderstands that.

"I'm in. What did you have in mind? Hiking? Bike ride? The swimming pool?"

I'm stop for a second. Why not? It wouldn't hurt to have someone to go with.

I write that I want to go on a bicycle tour to a nearby lake and less than five minutes later, I send him my address so that he can wait with his bicycle at my door.

I quickly take a shower, get ready and then stand in front of my wardrobe. For the date at the café I would have chosen the pretty white summer dress and sandals. But for a bike tour this is rather impractical, so I choose the tight shorts and a breathable t-shirt. It's not my favorite outfit, but at least its very figure hugging and therefore quite sexy anyways.  Instead of perfume I spray myself generously with a sunscreen spray and insect repellent and then slip into my sneakers.

I throw my bikini and a towel into my backpack and hope that I can change somewhere there.

Just as I am pouring water into my bottle, the doorbell rings. He's right on time, something I really appreciate.

I grab my stuff and walk down the stairs. When I open the door, he's standing right in front of it and smiling at me. He's wearing sunglasses, so I can't see everything from his face, but he looks nice, in fact, he looks a little better than in the photos.

"Hey, you're Anna?" He asks me and I nod.

"Nice to meet you. I'm Hanno!" He hesitates a bit, probably wondering whether to shake my hand or hug me. I make the decision and hug him. Then I go to my bike and get ready.

"And where are we going?" He asks me.

I am of course prepared and have chosen a long and beautiful route that leads us to a small, hidden lake, where hopefully not many people will be.

"Sounds good. I'll follow you!"

We leave and our route takes us once through the town and then through smaller woods to a river, which we follow until we cross several fields and eventually reach the lake.

It's hot now, the sun is beating down and I'm sweating, Hanno is too. He sees the glittering water, takes off his t-shirt and jumps in with his shorts.

"It is glorious! Come in!" He shouts to me before he disappears.

I'm looking around. We're alone here, so I could easily change. But I can't get completely naked on a first date.

"What?!" He shouts.

"I have to change," I answer honestly.

"You got nothing on underneath?"

"No. It's in my backpack."

"Then hurry up!"

He turns around and lies on his back to float on the water. Again I look around and decide to go a little further away from the shore. Hidden under a towel I try to put on my bikini but it is hopeless. Again and again the cloth blows up and he can surely see everything. Eventually I don't care and throw the towel and my T-shirt to the side and quickly put on my bikini top.

When I get back to the lake he's still floating on the water. Either he didn't see anything or he's pretending not to so he doesn't embarrass me.

I dive into the water and enjoy the cooling off before I see that Hanno has swum to me. He stands right in front of me and looks at me. He doesn't say a word but approaches me more and more intently. I wonder what's coming next; does he want to kiss me? But instead he claps his hands on the surface of the water and splashes me wet.

We fool around a bit before we go back to our bikes and spread out on the blankets and towels we brought with us.

"Glorious here," he says and stretches out to look at the blue sky. We lie next to each other for a while and don't say a word before we start chatting.

Eventually, he stands up again to look at me, I do the same and we look at each other again. This time there is no water to wet me with, instead we kiss. It's a very careful and gentle one kiss, rather hesitant. But it's a good kiss, and I want more. So I straighten up further so that I can wrap an arm around him and keep kissing him.

He then pulls me closer to him and at some point I sit on his lap with my legs apart. We make out extensively before our hands go on a discovery tour. Soon I have his right hand on my bottom, while the other one is on the front of my breasts and massages them. Again and again he pulls at my hard nipples, which regularly makes me moan.

We forgot everything around us and in between we didn't even look if we were alone at all. As I take a short breath and take a deep breath I look around and fortunately there is nobody around. Hanno presses me down on the blanket so that I now lie with my flat back on it.

40

He pulls on the straps of my bikini panties so that they come loose and he can simply put the piece of fabric aside.

"What are you doing?" I ask and look around again.

"Nobody's coming," he just says and pushes me back up. He holds my legs by my ankles, pulls them wide apart and then bends down to lick me.

Mmm... That feels good. His soft, warm tongue runs over my clitoris again and again with some pressure before he sucks and sucks on it. He goes on. Pulls his tongue once completely through my wet lips and then focuses on penetrating me with his tongue. Greedily he presses his tongue inside me and fucks me with it a little bit before he puts it back on my clit.

I feel I'm coming, my legs are shaking, and my stomach is tense. Hanno continues to hold me tight, presses his tongue on my clitoris and now licks quickly over it; this makes me come. I groan loudly, bend my body and push him away from me. I am especially sensitive shortly after the climax and for a few minutes I can't stand any touching. But he does not let go. His hands still lie on my legs and after I can breathe calmly again, he plays with his fingers on me again. He spreads my pussy and licks again with his tongue over my clit. Then he wanders deeper to my entrance and then a little deeper, over the dam and then down to my other hole. With pleasure he licks around it, moistens it and then presses his tongue into me.

I haven't experienced this before, but it feels good. It tickles slightly, but in a pleasant way. Again I close my eyes and enjoy what he does to me.

Then I feel a finger and how it carefully presses against my sphincter muscle to loosen it.

Very gently the first finger penetrates me and licks me further. Again through my lips and my clitoris, while he continues to finger my ass.

I feel more pressure now. He pushes another finger inside me and then continues. I start going mad with lust and can hardly stand it any longer; he touches me so well!

And then I'm coming, one more time, more intense and louder than before.

My whole body trembles and this time Hanno leaves me to rest for a short moment. He lies down next to me, observes how I try to breathe more calmly and grins at me when I open my eyes again.

"That was good," I say, and now I look down at him.
His shorts are baggy and I have a great desire to
return the favor.

So I stand up and I push him down on the blanket for
it. Greedily I push his only garment off his hip
and stare at his cock. It's big, thick and long and.
Incredibly. Hard.

With my fingers I carefully run over him, glide over
his tip, over the shaft and over his balls, before I take
him firmly in my hand and jerk off briefly. Then I
bend down to him. I watch very carefully how the
skin keeps retracting while I work on him with my
hand and then I put my mouth oh him. First I run my
soft, moist lips over his glans and shaft before I
stretch out my tongue and run it everywhere as well.

I now concentrate on its tip and keep licking it with
my tongue. Then I open my mouth and let his cock
slowly slide in as far as I get it and then I pull back
and repeat the whole thing.

I go up and down a few times with my mouth, suck
on it and play with my tongue.

I can hear Hanno breathing louder. He's moaning
now and has his eyes closed. His hands rest on my
shoulder and on my head, which he now pushes up
and down slightly again and again.

I adapt to his pace and become faster. With one hand I hold on to his cock and my mouth tightens around his beating. He breathes even faster. He's probably coming. I keep moving my hand up and down and my mouth is still tight around his cock.

And then he pulls his hands away, holds them to his head and then he comes. I watch his juice pour over my hand and I look at him satisfied.

He lies still. His chest rises and falls significantly and then he takes one deep breath.

"That was great," he says, looking for a towel to clean him and myself again.

I lie down next to him and we both stare at the blue sky.

All of a sudden he gets up and screams, "Last one in the water!" and runs off.

I completely forget that I am not wearing a bikini anymore and run after him naked. We fool around a little bit until one moment he pulls me into his arms and kisses me. He pushes me up by my thighs so that I can wrap my arms and legs around him and sit on his hips. We keep kissing until he runs off and takes me back to the beach. He puts me down on the blanket and continues kissing me. His hands go between my legs and he starts fingering me. First he circles my clit before he puts two fingers deep inside me and fucks me with them. Then he pulls them out again and puts them on my tight hole. Also there he pushes them in effortlessly while his head slides along my body again until he has reached between my legs again. He starts to lick me and I get wetter and wetter. But this time his fingers are not reaching me and I want more.

Carefully I turn around and stretch my ass out to him. I look at him over my shoulder and grin; he understands immediately and straightens up. He now kneels right behind me with has his hard cock in his hand. Then he slides closer, holding my hip with one hand while the other is still on his beating member.

I can feel him wetting my ass a little, then moving closer with his cock.

I try to relax and concentrate only on the horny feeling, which he triggers in me immediately. Carefully he presses his cock against my tight hole, which slowly opens for him. And then I feel him, the slight stretching pain, which I like so much it makes me moan. He presses in further until his thick member is completely inside me and then slowly let the rest follow.

Again I moan as he is completely inside me and fills me up like this. He starts to move after that, at first very slowly and carefully and then after I get used to his size, faster and harder.

It feels incredible to have such a thick beating beast inside me and I let my hand wander to my clitoris. I rub my pearl while he continues to push deep and hard inside me.

I close my eyes and place my head on my left hand, which is lying on the floor. My right hand continues to massage my clitoris.

"Harder," I tell him, and now he holds on to my hip with both hands. He pushes harder and harder and I feel goose bumps spreading over my body. Mmm... It feels so good, how hard he takes me from behind!

I keep rubbing and feel my stomach tighten. I'm almost there; if he goes a little faster then I know I'm going come.

Loudly I let my climax out, now claw myself with both hands in the ceiling, while he also starts for the finale. Faster and faster and harder he fucks me until he can't hold himself back either and comes half in my ass, half on it. Everything is full of his juice - I like that.

Exhausted, he lets himself fall down next to me and we both get deep pleasure before we turn on our backs again and stare up into the sky. Neither of us says a word. We are too overwhelmed by what has just happened.

I notice that I get very hungry and rummage in my bag for my mobile phone. It's way past noon. We've been here at the lake for four hours.

I put something on and dig out the cans I filled with fruit, vegetables and crackers from this morning. Satisfied, we go over the goodies and get dressed again afterwards.

"I looked at you, of course, when you changed your clothes earlier," he confesses to me with a grin.

"And that's when I realized I couldn't keep my hands off you today." Laughing, I shake my head. I knew it!

We get our bikes ready and then we start our way home. But not without taking a few more breaks in which he licks me and takes me again leaning against a tree from behind.

When I let myself fall exhausted on the couch in the evening and write with Hanno to plan the next meeting, everything hurts me, especially my butt, and not just from riding my bike.  It was all absolutely worth it.

# First Time at
# a Kinky Beats Party

I am sitting on the floor in my small single apartment and have a colorful shoebox in front of me. The box is filled with my 17-year-old memories, wishes and dreams, all of which I wrote just before my 18th birthday. The sides are closed with lots of tape and there are red crosses everywhere.

"Do not open until your 30th birthday," it says. I have to grin. Like a note would have stopped anyone from opening that box, but it did stop me. Today is my 30th birthday, which I would have thought would be a little more spectacular, with a huge party, DJ and everything. The closer I got to turning thirty, the less I felt like a party, so instead I insisted on quiet evening with some friends in my favorite bar.

The party ended an hour ago and now I sit here and cut through the thick tape with a knife.

I open the box and discover old photos of me with my best friends from school.

"I really want to be friends with Lisa, Anna and Caro when I am 30," I read and have to laugh again.
The friendship broke up after we moved to different cities to study, and since then I have only heard from them at Christmas. None of them have wished me a happy birthday. I discover more photos and then a list. A kind of bucket list of things I want to have experienced by my 30th birthday.

In the first place, "get married and have children" is the most important thing. Again, I laugh. I can't imagine marriage and kids, I'm still quite happy about my single life.

"Own a house, a dog, and a garden with swing," are also written on it. I have my own place, I guess that will have to do. I don't want to have a dog anymore since my ex-boyfriend's dog bit me and I get sick from the swings.

I turn the list over and there in pencil are a few things on it that I can hardly decipher. I probably didn't press very hard on it at the time so that I can't read it anymore.

"To have a threesome with two men. Go to a sex club. Let other watch me have sex. Make out with a woman." I reread the whole thing in amazement. I must have had a wild phase. I'm just trying to figure out when I checked those off, actually, just the last part; I know I did those already during my final exams. Otherwise ... no, I definitely haven't done the rest and it's got me thinking. Why not?

I go through my last relationships and when I look back, I was quite bored sexually. One time we had sex outside. One time we were thinking about getting another woman in, but other times...

I think back to when I was 17 years old. My brother had left the house shortly before and left me his laptop. When I went on the Internet to look for some clothes, I found his recently accessed pages. Among them of course were a bunch of porn sites.

Curiously I looked around there and in the following nights I watched all kinds of videos. At that time I was still a virgin, but I could imagine experiencing all this and I wished for a wild sex life.

It didn't really happen because my first boyfriend was a bit of a softie, and then I guess I kind of forgot about it all.

I am curious and go to my desk, where my laptop is. I try to remember the page and am amazed that it still exists. Even some of the videos from back then are still there. They are terribly bad quality and have hardly anything in common with the videos from today, but I still find them appealing. There are mainly couples that invite another man to their home, group sex or gang-bang scenes.

50

I look closely and eventually lose myself in all the videos. For a long time now I don't only look at the videos from back then, but also at newer ones, they're really quite something. I get horny and take my laptop with me to bed where I take out my favorite vibrator and pleasure myself.

When I lie in bed afterwards, satisfied, I think about my current life. It is beautiful but totally planned and predictable. My diary is full and every day after work I meet other friends for food or drinks on the weekends. Every Saturday I go shopping, clean the house and in the evening there is usually some birthday or other celebration of my friends. On Sundays I spend all day on the couch doing things I don't have time for otherwise.

In between there are of course free days and holidays. But even that is not really spectacular. I remember when I was seventeen. I imagined adult life very differently, my own car, wild parties every weekend and adventurous vacations.

Unfortunately reality is quite different.

I surf the Internet a little bit more and discover a link to "Germany's largest sex and erotic community" on the porn site. I get curious and follow the link. I land on a tasteful page and see the category "Events". Interested, I read the description and see the guest list. I expect an older audience over 50, like from the sex-reports that are shown on RTL at night, but here it looks different. The audience is younger, about my age, and even though as an unregistered viewer I can't see all the pictures, it appeals to me. It sounds like an ordinary electro party only with more open-minded attendees.

For years I have been imagining that I would go to such a party there has never been the right partner for it. Maybe I don't need a partner. Maybe I can join another group?

Quickly, I log on to the site, upload a photo before deciding to postpone the rest until tomorrow; I am tired and just want to sleep.

When I wake up the next morning and pick up my cell phone, I suddenly have several messages telling me that I have been contacted on the sex page. I quickly open my laptop and go through the messages.

Wow... one man after the other who wants to have sex with me without obligation. But that's not really what I was looking for. I answer everyone anyway and make it clear that I'm more looking for a group to go to one of the Kinky Beats parties happening soon near me. Of course I hope that someone can offer me exactly that.

Indeed I soon receive a message, from someone named Tom.

"We see regular attendees and although we're not a fixed group, many of us have known each other for a long time. Some of us don't come along anymore but newbies soon join to take their place. You are welcome to join us if you like," I read enthusiastically. That is exactly the right thing for me!

Tom and I arrange meet briefly for coffee beforehand. Going to a party with strangers is one thing, and I'd be more than happy to go but at a party of this kind I would like to clarify a few things first. I want to talk about what to wear as I've seen some pictures and leather seems very popular. Except for a tight leather skirt and a leather jacket I don't have anything like that in my closet.

We meet Sunday in a café around the corner, where I hope there will be so much going on that nobody can eavesdrop and understand what we are talking about.

I'm a little nervous and I show up punctually for the meeting, I can see him from afar. Except for the faceless pictures from his profile I don't know anything about him yet, but I already thought that he must be attractive and that turns out to be the reality.

He is one head taller than me, sporty, has dark hair
and light green eyes, which stand out clearly from his
rather darker complexion. He has a light beard and
wears a loose fitting outfit of jeans and a t-shirt.

"Hey, are you Sarah?" He asks me as he approaches. I
nod and immediately he opens his arms to greet me.

"Nice to meet you," he says, before we find a place in
the corner of the café.

We start chatting and he tells me about the process.
The group always meets before at someone's house,
usually it changes. This time it is his turn to play the
host, which of course feels nice to me. I'm grateful
I'm getting to know him before. They typically open
the night with drinks as they prepare for the evening
showing their outfits to each other.

"And what about you?" I ask him.

Of course, he has accumulated quite a lot of outfits
over the years and enumerates his various
pieces, which are mainly made of leather.

"And what's popular for women?" I want to know.

"Oh, they have a full selection, of course, and I'm
sure you have the right outfit in your closet." I shake
my head as I think of my skirt and jacket; it certainly
doesn't fit.
54

"You don't have any nice lingerie? Maybe a black bodysuit and fishnet stockings? Or sexy crop top? Or a short, tight dress?"

I start to think... "Yes, I do have something like that! I bought fishnet pantyhose back when everybody was wearing them under torn jeans and! I bought a bodysuit years ago too!"

"There you go! Sounds like your all set. Also, you can always change your clothes on location, so that we don't attract attention walking around half-naked. Basically it's like a normal party, the music is loud, everything is dark and there's alcohol and drinking. The difference is there are hidden rooms and corners where you can play secretly and you can even play in public. No bouncer will come and say that you can't give a blow job to the man you like on the dance floor and nobody will looks at you when you spread your legs and a someone comes between your legs," he says casually.

I listen with interest. It sounds so exciting and I really want to dive into this world and experience it all.

We chat for almost two hours before he has to leave again to visit his parents.

"So, see you on Saturday. 8 pm at my place. I'll text you the address in a minute," he says.

I also set off to meet a friend afterwards, but I cannot quite follow her words. I keep thinking about what Tom told me. Dark corners where you can play with each other and an open audience everywhere, who are not afraid to have sex on the dance floor.

The feelings continue for the rest of the week. I can't concentrate on work, sports or on meetings with my friends. With my mind on Saturday all the time, I stand in front of the mirror every single evening to check my outfits.

In the end, I ultimately bought something new. A beautiful black bodysuit with fine lace at the front and back and open sides held together with black straps. I feel sexy yet not too naked. For this purpose I bought hold-up stockings, which finish with a simple black waistband. I also bought new high heels, which hopefully are comfortable enough to dance all night long or do other things...

I put the bodysuit on before I go to Tom's and the stockings and shoes in a bag. Fortunately Tom does not live very far away from me, so close that I can even walk. As I stand in front of the house entrance and look for his bell sign, I realize how nervous I am. I hear the door opener, push the door open and then walk up the few steps to get to the open door.

56

"Hello, how are you?" Tom asks and spreads his arms out again to greet me.

He takes me to the apartment where there's already music playing. I enter the living room where nearly ten people turn to look at me and lift their glasses to greet me.

Tom shows me around, introduces me to everyone before he gives me my first drink.

"What are you going to wear?" Asks one of the women who is also there and knows that it is my first party like this.

I show her my bodysuit and tell her about my stockings.

"Sharp," she replies and nods approvingly.

A little later when we are ready to leave we are greeted by several taxi's waiting in front of the house ready to take us to the club. In the meanwhile I have relaxed a bit, which might have been assisted by the three gin and tonics I drank.

We join the long queue, pay and then come to a small locker area where we can change. I place my bag on a chair, take off my dress and then the stockings and shoes from my bag. I quickly put everything on and then look at the others in the group. The men mainly wear scarce pieces of spandex and leather. The women wear the most beautiful, sexy tight lingerie of artfully tied corsages, skin-tight full body suits and tight patent leather dresses.

"Ready?" Asks Tom, who is suddenly standing next to me.

I nod and we pass another control. Two people sit at another entrance and look at us very closely.

"What are they looking at?" I ask.

"They're just looking to see if your outfit is appropriate," he tells me.

He gives us all a nod and then we proceed through the wide door into a huge room. Half-naked people are standing everywhere, dancing and having fun.

"Do you want a drink?" I hear Tom ask, but I just shake my head. I want to look around and get my bearings. I've never seen anything like it.

At this very moment, a woman walks past me. She has two leashes in her hand leading to two men crawling on the ground behind her. I turn my head to the right, where two completely naked men are standing and talking to a woman wearing a bright red wig and nothing else.

"Will you dance with me?" Tom asks after he's had a beer. Dancing sounds good.

I follow the group, which now consists of only four people, and squeeze myself between Tom and a strange man.

I close my eyes, feel the music and start to move.

Suddenly I feel hands on me and I'm sure it's Tom. I keep my eyes closed, turn around so that I am now standing directly in front of him and press myself against his. My bottom is now rubbing against his cock and I am having fun doing it here so publicly on the dance floor.

Out of the corner of my eye I see the hands around my waist, one moving up and one moving down. One is now lying on my breasts while the other one can now reach into my crotch. I close my eyes again and continue dancing.

Suddenly I get tapped from the side and I look up immediately. It's Tom telling me that they're going outside for a moment.

Startled, I turn around. This is not Tom behind me, but the strange man who danced next to Tom! He smiles at me questioningly. He's cute and I am in the mood so I turn around again and keep rubbing my body against his.

His hands move to my hip again and we move together in rhythm. At some point I turn around again and look up at him. He smiles and not two seconds later he's pulled my face towards his to kiss me. I know these kinds of kisses, the demanding type that make you want more, that's is exactly what they do for me.

I cling to his shoulder and his hip and press my body firmly against his. He's not wearing much, so I can clearly feel his bump. His hands wander along my body. One is still on my head, while the other one is sliding over my back, down to my ass and then starts to knead it.

Suddenly he stops, grabs my hand and then pulls me behind him. I don't even ask him where he wants to take me, but instead just let it happen.

We land on a platform above the bar. some people dance here while the majority sit on stools, chatting or making out with each other. We find two free seats and before I turn my attention back to him, I look around a bit. Next to me are two women and a man kneels in front of them. With one hand he fingers one woman while licking the other. They moan and cling to their stools and don't even notice how they attracted the attention of some interested observers.

Then I hear loud moaning from a dark corner followed by heavy clapping.
"There are two fucking," says the strange man next to me, who then lays my legs in his lap.

The moaning gets louder and I see more and more people rushing there to watch what is happening. I am also about to check it out, but then I feel fingers between my legs, he fingers me. Now I can't possibly leave.

I turn my face back to his and see him cheekily grinning at me. We kiss again as he now pushes his fingers deep inside me, hitting exactly the right spot. I lay my face on his shoulder and enjoy what he does to me.

Quietly I start moaning, close my eyes and when I open them again a little later, I see the couple next to us grinning at me knowingly. She also sits on her partner's lap and he does the same with his fingers.

It feels great to watch others and to be watched while at my peak.

He now circles with his fingers around my clitoris and that takes me to climax. I'm coming.
Carefully he pulls his hand back again and waits until my climax has subsided.

"Do you want to sit on my dick?" He asks directly.

And how I'm up for that!

He helps me up, pushes his pants down and I stare at his hard, big cock.

Carefully I sit down on him, let him slide into me and then start to move. I feel the looks in my back. Not only the couple next to us is watching intently, but other's as well. They voyeurs don't bother me, on the contrary, they spur me on to go faster and ride him even harder.

I ride myself to my second orgasm and a little later he also comes.

Radiantly he looks at me as I slow down and carefully get off him again.

This is exactly how I imagined my first visit here.

We go to the toilet and have a drink at the bar before we go back to the dance floor and let the night fade away.

I don't see the group anymore. Not until the next morning, when Tom writes to me and asks if I will be back next time. Oh yes, I'll definitely be back.

# A Gangbang
## with Strangers

I t is Friday night when I look at my cell phone bored and hoping some emergency will come in. I ask for a burst pipe at the neighbors', a break-in at my parents' or something that could save me from this terrible date. The display is blank and I sigh, there is no emergency. Annoyed, I watch my date Ralf come back to the table.

"So where were we? Oh, right. My latest project..." he starts and tells me about some tractors and machines I have no idea about. I squint at the clock, It's only 9 pm. I've only spent an hour with him, but it feels like at least ten.

"So... I have to get up early tomorrow. Shall we pay?" I ask hopefully, even though I know it's rude. He hasn't even finished eating.

"Oh. Where do you have to go so early on a Saturday?" He wants to know. I push around, trying to think of something fast... Pipe burst! Yeah, right.

"My parents recently had a burst pipe in their house, I'll have to help out tomorrow. A lot of things have been broken," I say and take on a depressed look.

"Oh, I see. Yeah, I know that one. In my company ..." he starts talking again and mentions some machines I can't do anything with. I roll my eyes and look at the waiter looking for help, he gives me a pitiful look.

I quickly reach out my hand and wave to him.

"If he's ever around..." I explain to Ralf and ask for the bill.

Finally we pay and leave the restaurant a little later.

"So, this was really nice with you. I hope we can do this again," he says and I just grin.

"Yes, of course..." I reply. Of course I don't mean it.

"Since you're busy tomorrow, how about Sunday? I could," he suggests.

"Oh Ralf... I'm at my parents' all weekend and the week after there's a super important project coming up. It will be hard to squeeze you in, but of course I'll try. I'll get in touch with you," I lie and then turn the other way. Hopefully he will understand that at least.

"Okay, I'm expecting your call." He calls after me, but by then I'm already a few meters away from him.

When I turn into the side street where I don't really have to go, I stop and look at my mobile phone again. There's a message from my friend Tine, who wants to know how it went.

"Catastrophe!" I only answer.

"Oh, I'm sorry. Will you tell me everything tomorrow? At lunch?" she writes, and I resent having to cancel on her for tonight because of that loser.

"Sure." I write, and then I put the phone away. I look around. I've never been in this neighborhood. Actually I would have had to go the other direction, but Ralf wanted to go there as well and I didn't want to spend another second with him.

I see a couple of bars and I immediately get the urge for a cocktail. But alone? Hmm... I approach the bar and look through the window at all the people sitting there in groups. Nah, I'm not that desperate after all.

"Hey, are you here alone?" I'm suddenly asked and I turn around. A man about my age, in his late 20s or early 30s, stands before me. Behind him are other men waiting for him.

"Yes, but actually I was just leaving," I answer.

"Where to?"  He wants to know.

"Home"…?

He demonstratively takes out his cell phone to check his watch, "At 9 pm? Bad date or something?"

I laugh, "You got me, you got me."

"And that's what you let it ruin your evening?! Come and join us," he says and actually, he is right. I was looking forward to the weekend for so long and shouldn't let a bad date spoil my mood.

"Okay," I say, and I get closer to the group.

"I'm Marvin and these are my friends," he says, pointing to the four men who nod at me in encouragement.

"Jenny," I say, waving to everyone.

We enter the pub and quickly find a free seat.

"What do you want to drink?" Marvin asks. I decide on a mojito, and then another, and another and then come the shots and finally my spirits go up.

At that point I join in on the songs that are playing and let myself go completely.

By the time the pub closes we are the last ones to leave the shop.

"Now what?" asks one of Marvin's buddies. Nobody wants to go home yet but the city center and therefore the next pubs are too far away.

"I live nearby," I say. "And I still have plenty of booze at home."

Everybody cheers and then we start running. Probably not the best idea to take five complete strangers home, but I don't want this night to end.

When we arrive at my place, everyone makes themself comfortable on my sofa; fortunately, it's big enough. I dig out a couple of open bottles of liquor from the fridge and prepare six shot glasses. Then someone suggests that we have a drinking game.

"Only eighteen year olds do that!" Protests one, but I'm quite taken with the idea.

I would have been against it once too, because the games are only aimed at me telling the men all my dirty sex secrets. When I had my first time, how many sex partners I've had since, how many toys I own and my preferences that even my best friend doesn't know.

"And what would you like to try?" Someone asks.

In the meantime, I have had so much alcohol that I am not even embarrassed to blurt it all out.

"A gangbang. I want a really wild gangbang like in the pornos, several men and me. They take me through it all, they squirt their juices into all of my orifices and then they go right on. They hold me tight, push hard and only stop when none of them can do anymore," I tell them, not noticing how the five of them stare at me with interest.

"Mmm... interesting," finally one of them says.

"And how badly do you want to try this?"

"Oh, it's urgent. So if the opportunity arose, I probably wouldn't say no."

"And what would you say if you had the chance now?"

Surprised, I look at the questioner, and then the rest of the group. No one seems surprised, they probably they do it often.

"Um," I press around. It's not like I can say no now. I think about it and I look at them again. They're all attractive and really good-looking, I don't think I could do any better.

"Yes, well..." I start to make up an excuse. But why? I wished for this, and with them I could really imagine it. Besides, all this talk about sex has made me horny as hell.

"Yes. I'd say yes," I finally answer.

"Excellent!" Marvin gets up and pulls me up to his place. Before I could say anything else, I have his lips on mine and he kisses me.

The other men follow and suddenly I have numerous hands on my body. At first I remain tense, but when he lets go of me again and looks at me, I suddenly relax, because I see the lust in his eyes, which somehow transfers to me.

The men clear the glass table with all the bottles to the side and fold the sofa down so that we have a large lying area. Afterwards Marvin undresses me and I see the rest of the group following. Soon I am standing in the middle of five naked men, all greedily staring at me.

"Marvin gets the right of way," says one of them and he approaches me while holding his hard cock in his hand massaging it. I decide to join in and enjoy it all. I don't think about how strange all this is, I just want to enjoy it.

So I get down on my knees, stretch out my hand for his beating member and lead him into my mouth. Immediately his hands find themselves on my head and press him against his pelvis.

Yeah, okay. That's the way I wanted it, hard and without regard for me. He puts that into practice now. He takes my hair to a ponytail and fucks my neck while the other men approach me. They lift me up and a little later I find myself on the sofa in the quadruped stand. Marvin is still standing right in front of me with his cock in my mouth.

I can't turn my head and so I can't see how many of the men are now behind me, but I feel hands everywhere. On my breasts, on my ass and on my pussy, which is now being fingered hard.

The hands change and I feel a stabbing pain on my bottom. Someone has struck with the flat of his hand. I flinch and squint my eyes together while someone notices that it just made me even wetter.

I try to moan, but the cock in my mouth keeps me from doing so.

Suddenly Marvin withdraws and I can take a deep breath through my mouth. It's not long before another man takes his place.

I concentrate on the hard cock in my mouth while fingers continue to drill into my holes. Two in my pussy and two in my ass to prepare me for what's about to follow.

And then everyone withdraws again. I feel hands on my hips and then something hard against my clit. Without warning, a huge cock now presses itself into my pussy and immediately starts to fuck me hard. I grab hold of the sofa, keep my mouth open and enjoy how these men use me. How one after the other penetrates me, how they do with me what they want. It feels really great to be their toy.

I hear moaning. It's the man whose dick is in my mouth right now. A little later I taste his juice and want to spit it out, but he holds my face.

"Swallow it nice," he says and only lets me go again when he sees that everything is gone.

"Good girl." He pats my head and makes room for the next one.

A change has also taken place in the back. Another man has come and again I feel hands, but this time on my ass. Once again fingers are pushed deep into my tight hole and they move, pull apart and then come back again.

A cock is attached and very slowly a big acorn pushes itself into my ass.

Again I try to groan and again it is not possible because a cock bores itself deep into my neck and fucks inexorably.

And then I flinch. I feel fingers on my clitoris. They rub and squeeze it as the cock shoves itself deeper and deeper into my ass. It pauses for a moment before it begins to move slowly inside me only to accelerate with each thrust just like the rubbing of my pearl.

I can feel everything contracting inside of me. My legs tighten and my stomach too. The blows are getting faster and faster and then I come. I flinch and hear the men cheering because they have brought me to my first orgasm, but they don't stop, they keep going. I would like to take a little breather, but the pushes get faster and harder.

Another man comes and again I swallow his juice. I feel the twitch in my ass and know that he must have come too.

The seats will be changed again. This time my mouth remains free, instead someone sits down under me and now I am to sit on his cock.

Very deeply my body is pushed forward so that I lie flat on his chest while my ass is stretched upwards.
72

I know what they're up to now and then I feel it too, another beating cock on my asshole. Carefully the tip pushes itself into me and I see how tense everybody is looking to see if it fits. I bite my lips when I feel the pressure, this would be my first time if it really works.

And then I hear a cheering again and feel a hard cock slipping into my stretched hole.

Strong hands hold me down and then they start to fuck me, first very slowly and alternately and then faster and faster and simultaneously.

The feeling is incredible. It feels so rotten and yet so horny. I feel the two cocks so intensely in me that I think I will come again in a moment.

"Harder! Faster," I call and I hear everyone laughing!

"It was clear that she likes this a lot," says one of them! The grip on my ass gets a bit tighter and I feel the pushes very hard inside me now.

In fact, it won't be long before I come again.

Through my twitching and contraction another man also comes and I feel his juice land on my back and run down my body. He retreats, but my ass does not stay empty for long, because then the next one comes.

I don't know how long this will go on, but the men seem to be tireless and come more than once or twice. I have come more times and have who knows how much sperm in and on my body. I feel how I am slowly getting tired and can hardly find the strength for further highlights but they just keep on coming. Sometimes it is only one who fucks me in the mouth, in the pussy or in the ass. Sometimes it's two at the same time. Last time I even had three cocks in me. They've already fucked me in all sorts of positions on the floor, on the sofa or on the table.

My ass and my pussy feel incredibly sore and I will certainly remember this day for a long time as soon as I want to sit down, but for now there seems to be no end in sight.

"Are you holding up?" Marvin asks me. I want to shake my head, but I don't want this night to end either, it's just way too awesome.

"Fine," he just says and then pushes me down on the floor with my knees to push his cock in my mouth, which he had in my ass before but it doesn't even bother me. It makes me kind of horny to go along with whatever they come up with for me.

He comes and then helps me up. I look around. The other men are in the kitchen drinking water.

"They'll only take a short break before continuing on."

He also hands me a glass. But I only manage one sip before it is torn out of my hand again and I am pressed over the back of the sofa. A hard cock penetrates my ass and fucks me. My body forces me to have another orgasm and then everything just feels like in a trance. One last time I am placed on the lap of a man before another man enters me from behind.

The others cheer the two of them to fuck me even harder and harder and then they come.

I'm shaking all over and trying to get along. They leave me alone and I hear Marvin's voice in my head.

"You held out well," he says and caresses my body.

"Where is the bathroom?"

I point to a white door beside the sofa and feel his hand on my arm. He pulls me up by it and puts me in the shower.

"You've been hit hard," I hear him say as he turns on the water.

I still manage to take a shower on my own, even if I have trouble keeping upright on my legs, which feel totally soft.

I wrap myself in a big towel and come back to the living room. The men have already cleaned up and dressed.

I see Marvin holding his phone up.

"Can I have your number in case you feel the call again?" He asks.

I cannot yet imagine when I may again want a cock in me, but in any case I don't want this horny experience to remain unique.

I try to remember my number and type it into his cell phone.

Everyone waves to me before they leave my apartment and I let myself fall naked into my cuddly bed. When I cannot fall asleep immediately, I notice that it is bright in my bedroom. The sun is shining through my window, because it is already the next morning.

Wow... what a night.